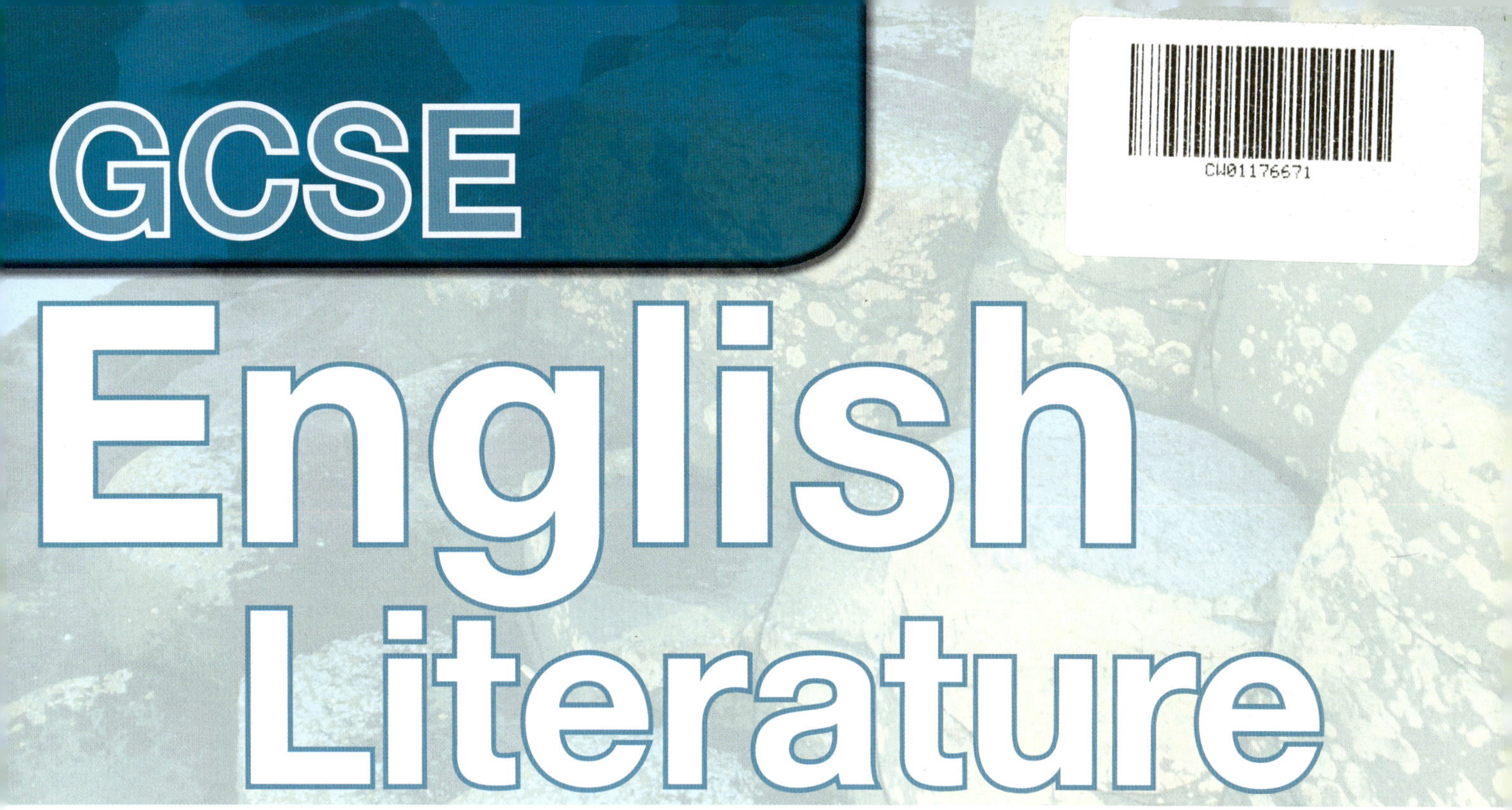

GCSE English Literature for CCEA

Authors:
Conor Macauley
Fiona Verner

Contents

Introduction	iv
The English Literature specification at a glance	v
How this book is structured	v
Foundation tier and Higher tier	vi
Assessment Objectives	vi
Moving up the grades	vii

Unit 1: The Study of Prose — 2

Introduction	2
1 Setting	7
2 Plot	11
3 Theme	15
4 Character	19
5 Language and style	23
6 Bringing it all together	28
Things Fall Apart by Chinua Achebe	32
Lord of the Flies by William Golding	34
The Power and the Glory by Graham Greene	36
To Kill a Mockingbird by Harper Lee	38
Animal Farm by George Orwell	40
Of Mice and Men by John Steinbeck	42

Unit 2: The Study of Drama and Poetry — 44

Section A: Drama — 44

Introduction	44
1 Plot and structure	50
2 Characterisation	54
3 Stage directions and dramatic techniques	58
4 Themes	62
5 Use of language	66
6 Bringing it all together	70
Dancing at Lughnasa by Brian Friel	74
All My Sons by Arthur Miller	76
Juno and the Paycock by Sean O'Casey	78
An Inspector Calls by J.B. Priestley	80
Blood Brothers by Willy Russell	82
Macbeth by William Shakespeare	84
Romeo and Juliet by William Shakespeare	86
The Merchant of Venice by William Shakespeare	88

Unit 2: The Study of Drama and Poetry — 90

Section B: Poetry — 90

Introduction	90
Two new skills	92

Anthology 1: Love and Death — 96
'Ozymandias' by P.B. Shelley — 96
'A Poison Tree' by William Blake — 98
'The Five Students' by Thomas Hardy — 100
'La Belle Dame sans Merci' by John Keats — 102
'Bredon Hill' by A.E. Housman — 104
'The Cap and Bells' by W.B. Yeats — 106
'Out, Out' by Robert Frost — 108
'Piazza Piece' by John Crowe Ransom — 110
'Richard Cory' by Edwin Arlington Robinson — 112
'Night of the Scorpion' by Nissim Ezekiel — 114
'Those Winter Sundays' by Robert E. Hayden — 116
'Love Song: I and Thou' by Alan Dugan — 118

Anthology 2: Nature and War — 122
'The Attack' by Siegfried Sassoon — 122
'An Irish Airman Foresees His Death' by W.B. Yeats — 124
'The Field of Waterloo' by Thomas Hardy — 126
'Auguries of Innocence' by William Blake — 128
'Westminster Bridge' by William Wordsworth — 130
'The Badger' by John Clare — 132
'The Castle' by Edwin Muir — 134
'In Westminster Abbey' by John Betjeman — 136
'The Battle' by Louis Simpson — 138
'Death of a Naturalist' by Seamus Heaney — 140
'A Narrow Fellow in the Grass' by Emily Dickinson — 142
'Foxes among the Lambs' by Ernest Moll — 144

Anthology 3: Seamus Heaney and Thomas Hardy — 148
'Thatcher' by Seamus Heaney — 148
'Blackberry Picking' by Seamus Heaney — 150
'At a Potato Digging' by Seamus Heaney — 152
'Last Look' by Seamus Heaney — 154
'An Advancement of Learning' by Seamus Heaney — 156
'Trout' by Seamus Heaney — 158
'The Old Workman' by Thomas Hardy — 160
'Wagtail and Baby' by Thomas Hardy — 162
'A Sheep Fair' by Thomas Hardy — 163
'At Castle Boterel' by Thomas Hardy — 164
'An August Midnight' by Thomas Hardy — 166
'Overlooking the River Stour' by Thomas Hardy — 168

Unit 2: The Study of Drama and Poetry — 172

Section C: Unseen Poetry — 172
Bringing it all together — 172
Sample unseen poems — 174

Glossary of terms — 185
Acknowledgements — 186

Introduction

This Student's Book has been designed to meet the examination demands (Units 1 and 2) of the CCEA General Certificate of Secondary Education in English Literature.

You can access the specification on www.ccea.org.uk and any changes to the specification will be published on this website. The version on the website will always be the most up-to-date version so this is the best place to go to check the specification.

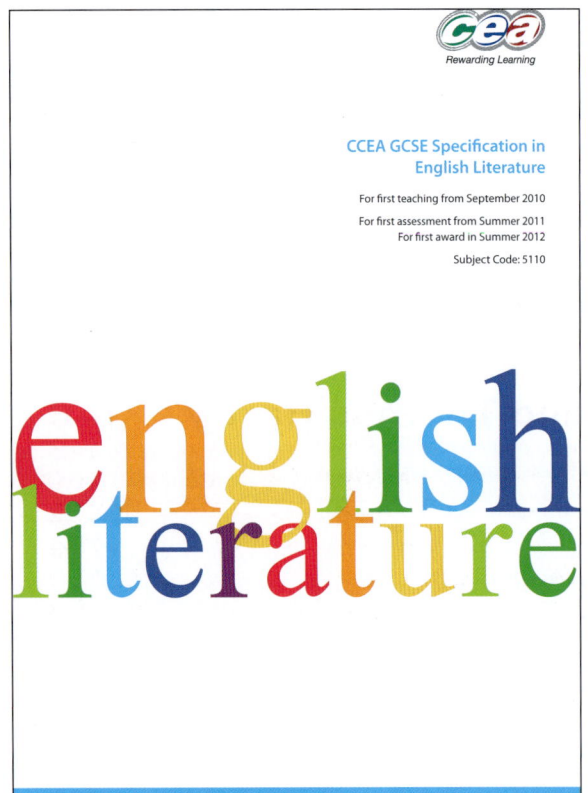

This Student's Book is intentionally narrow in its focus. It does not refer explicitly to the CCEA English Language specification, although the specifications for English Language and English Literature are fully compatible with each other. Nor does it refer to the Controlled Assessment element of the English Literature course as our concern here is preparing you for that part of the course which is externally assessed – Units 1 and 2.

Although the material is firmly grounded in the GCSE English Literature specification, we were mindful of the needs of students who wish to proceed to study the subject at AS or A2 Level.

The English Literature specification at a glance

Content	Assessment	Weighting	Availability
Unit 1: The Study of Prose	External examination Foundation and Higher tiers 1 hour	25%	Every summer (beginning in 2011)
Unit 2: The Study of Drama and Poetry	External examination Foundation and Higher tiers 2 hours	50%	Every summer (beginning in 2012)
Unit 3: The Study of Linked Texts	Controlled Assessment CCEA will set the task each year.	25%	Every summer (beginning in 2012)

Note that at least 40 per cent of the assessment (based on unit weightings) must be taken at the end of the course as terminal assessment.

How this book is structured

This Student's Book has four sections, corresponding to the four examination questions which you will answer – Prose, Drama, Poetry and the Unseen Poem. In this new, 'unitised' specification, you will be able to take any of the three units at the end of the first year of teaching, but we guess that the Prose unit (Unit 1) is the one you are most likely to take early. So we have sequenced the book to match the order of the units in the specification, since this is the order in which you are most likely to encounter the material in examinations.

The examination counts for 75 per cent of the total marks, the remaining 25 per cent being devoted to Controlled Assessment (Unit 3). Note that Controlled Assessment is not discussed in this book, which is concerned with the external examination units only – Units 1 and 2.

In the Prose section (Unit 1) and Drama section (Unit 2: Section A), there are a series of chapters discussing aspects of the genre – structure, characterisation, and so on. Each of these chapters contains activities where in writing and discussion you can engage with relevant aspects of the text you are studying. The chapter 'Bringing it all Together', refers in turn to each of the set texts, and contains sample material, examiner comments and advice on how to approach the various types of question that you may be asked.

In the Poetry unit (Unit 2: Section B) you will find your chosen Anthology discussed poem by poem, with questions on the poems, and suggestions about how to write about theme and style.

The final section of the book deals with the Unseen Poem (Unit 2: Section C), mainly through practice items for Foundation and Higher tiers.

Foundation tier and Higher tier

Although this Student's Book is aimed more directly at Higher tier students, as the questions at this tier have no bullet points and the requirement to plan an answer is more urgent, it is fully usable if you are entering at Foundation tier too. In the Unseen Poem section (Unit 2: Section C), where the question types differ radically between tiers, examples of both question types are given.

These icons are used to identify Foundation or Higher tier questions:

 Foundation tier   Higher tier

Assessment Objectives

The Assessment Objectives are rarely mentioned in this Student's Book – and yet they are its informing influence. You are probably more interested in the texts you are studying than in documents such as specifications and Mark Schemes, and we believe that if properly designed questions are asked in the examination, you can be expected to produce answers which meet the Assessment Objectives. The relevant AOs for each section are given on pages 31, 73, 92 and 173. The Assessment Objectives are also listed in the specification and in the Specimen Assessment Materials Booklet.

Nevertheless, even a cursory glance through this book will show you the importance of AO2 – the understanding of the writer's technique. If any Assessment Objective can be said to drive the examination, it is this. Most students present themselves for this examination with sufficient knowledge of the texts but with some, their understanding may be superficial. Understanding the novelist's or dramatist's or poet's technique is assessed in every question of the examination so a good grasp of the skills involved is essential to enable you to move up the grades. One of the aims of the English Literature specification is mastering transferable skills: the Assessment Objectives are **skills** to be learned and used in a variety of situations. This is why we have included samples of student responses to exam questions through the book. These samples show the skills at various stages of development.

Moving up the grades

On many pages of this Student's Book there are references to how you can improve performance in your essays. There may be a 'Moving up the grades' heading or there may be a mention of Mark Bands. If you look at page 120 you will see a table (known as an Assessment Grid). This lists the skills you may display in your answer in a number of columns. These columns are known as bands. Your aim over the two-year course is to develop the skills that will move you consistently from a lower to a higher Mark Band. As you use this book, you will be continually reminded of this by the repetition of key words such as 'focus', 'development', 'writer's technique'. This is done to encourage you to produce the best answer you are capable of, and to become more conscious of where and how to apply the effort required to enable you to do this.

Good students are sometimes described by examiners as being able to 'think on their feet'. They read the question carefully, without trying to twist it to mean something more convenient, maybe something they have already practised in class. They deal with what the question means, not with what they want it to mean, and they choose the material which is relevant, not the material that they are most comfortable with. That is what we hope that this book will enable you to do. We also hope that you will enjoy the English Literature course and using this book.

Acknowledgement

We would like to acknowledge a debt to the writers of *GCSE English Literature for CCEA* (Hodder and Stoughton 2007) – John Andrews, Len Quigg and Pauline Wylie – some of whose ideas for activities and layout we have gratefully used.

Unit 1

The Study of Prose

Introduction

Studying prose texts

While the study of a GCSE English Literature novel should ideally develop a natural enjoyment of the storyline, success in this examination does not solely depend on how well you 'know the story'. Knowing the story *is*, however, a good start, laying the foundation on which you can develop all the other skills involved in analysing a prose text.

You will need to consider some important questions:

- Why did the author write this novel?
- What themes or issues did the author want to explore?
- What techniques did the author use in writing this novel?

You have to be able to identify and comment on the various skills and techniques used by the writer to make the story interesting and effective, such as character development and use of language.

In other words, when studying a novel for examination you are expected to show close engagement with all aspects of that text and show an understanding of the writer's purpose and skills.

Key features of prose texts

First, you need to have a thorough knowledge and understanding of the text. This will come from classroom experiences, personal study, essay practice and revision, and possibly internet research. If you are going to discuss and evaluate a novel thoroughly, the most important aspects are:

- **Plot** – the sequence of events that forms the storyline
- **Themes** – the important issues that the author wants to explore
- **Characters** – and the relationships between them, and how they develop
- **Setting** – the situation in which the story takes place
- **Language and style** – use of dialogue, imagery, various types of language.

These key features will be considered in more detail in the following chapters and there will be comments on the novel you are studying.

What kind of questions will be asked?

In the Prose unit (Unit 1), you will be assessed on your:

- knowledge and understanding of the novel you have studied
- understanding of the techniques the writer has used.

Foundation or Higher tier? – An important choice

F Foundation tier questions are slightly more straightforward than Higher tier questions. They also provide more help as they include bullet points which direct you to relevant areas of the novel. The downside is that at Foundation tier the highest grade you can achieve is a Grade C.

H Higher tier questions are more complex. They may encourage you to look at both sides of an argument, or the question may have an additional part. Higher tier questions have no bullet points, so there is little guidance about relevant areas of the novel to discuss. (It is not true that there is *no* guidance, as we shall see when we unpack a Higher tier question.) At Higher tier you can be rewarded with a grade up to Grade A★.

The examiner does not want to surprise you. When you know the question types in advance, you are more likely to produce your best work.

You can compare sample Foundation tier and Higher tier questions in the 'Bringing it all together' section (pages 28–31).

Which question?

For each novel, there is a choice of questions. You may choose between writing a **character-focused** essay and a **theme-focused** essay.

The **(a)** question will ask for a **character-focused** essay. This should **not** be a general character 'sketch' or description. You must present your ideas about a character (or characters) in response to the specific question set.

The **(b)** question will ask for a **theme-focused** essay. You will have to present your ideas about a theme or issue in the text. You will already know from a detailed study of your novel what the main themes are.

Here are two questions on *Animal Farm*. At Foundation tier there will be bullet points to help you.

> **(a)** With reference to the ways Orwell **presents** Boxer, show how far you **admire** Boxer.

This question is not asking you to write a general description of Boxer's character. You should focus your answer on Boxer's admirable qualities.

> **(b)** Show that the Seven Commandments **fail** in the course of the novel.

Question **(b)** asks you to look at the theme of failure in the novel. The question, however, is specific – focus on the failure of the Seven Commandments, don't write about failure generally.

Extract or no extract?

The Prose unit (Unit 1) is a 'closed-book' examination. This means that you will not have a copy of the novel with you. So you cannot:

- search through the text to remind yourself of events and characters
- check quotations you wish to use.

You will have to rely on your knowledge of the text and ability to remember its features. A methodical revision programme leading up to the examination will help you.

However, one question, either **(a)** or **(b)**, will be based on an **extract** which you will receive along with the examination paper. It is important that you practise answering both kinds of question, so that in the exam you can choose the question that will give you the best chance to show your abilities.

Let's now consider the challenges and advantages of each question type – the **extract-based question** and the **free-standing essay**.

The extract-based question

Many students like an extract because they feel it gives them a starting point. Then, when they have 'settled in', they can move on to 'elsewhere in the novel'.

However, you must remember that a key word in the question is going to be **presents**, so the examiner is looking for your ideas about *how* the writer presents the material in the extract. You need to discuss in some detail things like **dialogue**, **language** and **imagery**, **paragraphing** or **punctuation**. Accurate and properly presented quotation from the extract is expected. You have been given the extract: it is up to you to use it!

In your answer you will need to **balance** use of the extract and 'elsewhere in the novel'.

F At Foundation tier, bullet points will help you to balance your answer and suggest an effective order for you to deal with the material.

H There are no bullet points at Higher tier so you will need to **plan your answer**, allowing time to deal with both extract and 'elsewhere in the novel'. You will also have to decide whether to start with the extract or not. To some extent, strong work in one area may compensate for less thorough work in another, but remember, both extract and 'elsewhere in the novel' need to be discussed in response to the specific question.

The free-standing essay

There is no extract to consider, so you may be able to make a quicker start, though you must remember how important it is to plan your answer.

F At Foundation tier, bullet points will help you to do this.

H At Higher tier there are no bullet points, and you may feel that there is very little support in the question. But this may not be true. Here is an example.

> **H** With reference to the ways Steinbeck **presents** George, show how far you would agree that George is a **true friend** to Lennie.

Examiner's tip!
The key terms will be printed in bold to help you.

This essay question does not tie you down to an extract, but gives you some freedom to select your own relevant material. You can choose whether to consider a limited amount of material in depth, or to write a broader essay which goes into less detail.

Considering the writer's skill and technique

What does 'presents' mean?

This key term is found in almost every question set. It directs you to discuss the techniques used by the writer to create all aspects of the story which we, as readers, enjoy.

Whichever question type you select, you *must* attend to the key term **presents**. With no extract, you will do this in a general way, discussing such features as characterisation, structure and contrast. Any relevant references or quotations you can provide are valuable. With an extract-based question, you can deal with the techniques the writer has used in the extract in a detailed way, and then refer to the techniques used 'elsewhere in the novel' in a more general fashion.

Here are some writer's techniques and uses of language to consider:

- **structure** of the text: e.g. chapters; use of climax; chronological ordering; flashback; introductions and conclusions; repetition, parallelism, comparison, contrast
- **descriptive techniques:** e.g. vocabulary choices; use of visual and aural imagery
- creation of **setting:** e.g. time; place; atmosphere
- creation of **character:** e.g. narrator's descriptions; use of dialogue; actions; interaction with others
- **narration:** e.g. omniscient narrator; first-person narrator; use of persona; autobiography
- use of **punctuation** and other **typographical effects:** e.g. italics; capitalisation; suspension points.

Discussing the writer's techniques in a way which is relevant to the question will put you on the road to success in the Prose unit (Unit 1) and in the English Literature examination generally.

The six set texts in the Prose unit (Unit 1)

In the Prose unit of the English Literature examination, the six set texts are:

- *Things Fall Apart* by Chinua Achebe (see pages 32–33)
- *Lord of the Flies* by William Golding (see pages 34–35)
- *The Power and the Glory* by Graham Greene (see pages 36–37)
- *To Kill a Mockingbird* by Harper Lee (see pages 38–39)
- *Animal Farm* by George Orwell (see pages 40–41)
- *Of Mice and Men* by John Steinbeck (see pages 42–43)

You are required to study **one** of these texts.

Setting 1

In the English Literature examination, you may be asked to write about 'characters, ideas, themes or settings'. In this section, we will look at what is meant by the setting of the novel you are studying.

Where and when

The setting is the background against which the characters carry out their actions. It is the place where the action happens, but also the historical time in which it happens. A novel can have more than one setting. We can speak of setting in a wide sense – a country for example; or in a narrow sense – a room. Settings can be based on a real time and place, such as 1930s Alabama in *To Kill a Mockingbird*, or they can be imaginary, such as the farm where animals can talk in *Animal Farm*. Or they can be a mixture of both.

> **Key Word**
> **Setting**
> The place and time of a story

Why are settings important?

We will look at three reasons why settings in a novel are important:

- to add to our understanding of character and action
- to create atmosphere
- to create contrast.

To add to understanding of character and action

A setting may help us understand what is happening, and also *why* it is happening. For example, in *Things Fall Apart* the life of the main character, Okonkwo, falls apart. It adds greatly to our understanding that the setting for this event is West Africa, that Europeans have just arrived in the area, and that they are determined to destroy and replace the tribal way of life. So we come to understand that the title refers to much more than just the life of Okonkwo.

Correspondingly, the way Steinbeck describes the 1930s setting in *Of Mice and Men*, with its unemployment, enforced travel, work-tickets and job interviews, helps us understand how an event like Lennie's death could happen, and why George felt as he did about it.

To create atmosphere

The setting can also be important in creating atmosphere. For example, *The Power and the Glory* begins with a description of a port town, with a 'little burnt plaza', a statue of an 'ex-human being', vultures looking for carrion, and a dirty, sluggish river. This creates an atmosphere of exhaustion and hopelessness, which is an important part of the meaning of the novel. Fortunately, the plot is an exciting one!

7

Consider the setting at the start of *Lord of the Flies*. The details of the description of the tropical island – the sunshine, the sand, the coral reef, the deep swimming pool on the beach – show why the boys who survived the plane crash become pleased and excited, believing that they are part of a great adventure.

To create contrast

Often, a writer will use contrasting settings, for example as Steinbeck does in *Of Mice and Men* when he moves from the natural surroundings of the pool, with the deep green river and the animals coming to drink, to the bare and comfortless bunkhouse where George and Lennie will live. Why does Steinbeck choose to do this? Perhaps he is showing us something about one setting by contrasting it with another which is very different. Perhaps also he is showing us something about the characters by describing how they act in differing environments.

Examiner's tip!
Try to understand *how* writers use settings and what their intentions are.

ACTIVITY 1
Considering setting

Complete these tasks for the novel you are studying.

1 In groups or with your teacher, select one setting from your novel which seems interesting and important (perhaps because an important event or a significant change took place there).

2 Make notes on how the writer describes the setting. Jot down important or memorable details.

3 Write a paragraph in which you:
- explain what part the setting plays in the novel and what happens there
- show how the writer uses language to describe the setting
- explain why you think this setting is important.

4 Read your paragraph to other members of the group. Share your group's ideas with the whole class.

ACTIVITY 2
Settings in *Things Fall Apart*

1 Collect and note down some of the words and phrases which Achebe uses to describe these settings.

2 Write two short paragraphs outlining the main events which occur in the marketplace and in Okonkwo's compound.

Reviewing the setting of your chosen novel

Things Fall Apart

Some key settings:

- the marketplace and *ilo* (playground) of Umuofia, where several important events take place. The village is centred here.
- Okonkwo's compound. His family life is centred here.
- the wider setting, the area of West Africa near the Lower Niger, with its huts, farms, dirt tracks, and scrub and forest land.

Lord of the Flies

The island is doubly enclosed by the calm waters of the lagoon and by the coral reef. The 'snapping sharks' wait far away outside the reef, and the war in the air is 10 miles above the boys' heads. 'This is a good island,' says Ralph.

ACTIVITY 3
Settings in *Lord of the Flies*

1. Why do you think Golding chose an island for the setting of his novel? Write a paragraph suggesting some reasons for his choice.
2. What are the important features of the geography of the island? Describe briefly what happens in each of the places you have mentioned.

The Power and the Glory

In this novel the setting is important as it helps create atmosphere. Greene emphasises the ugliness and depressingly run-down nature of the surroundings – whether he is describing the state capital or the outlying villages. 'This was the atmosphere of a whole state.'

ACTIVITY 4
Settings in *The Power and the Glory*

1. Why do you think Greene sets the main part of the novel in a run-down area? (Collect and be ready to use some of the words and phrases in these descriptions.)
2. Note the contrasting setting in Part 3 – the Lehrs' hacienda. Why do you think Greene makes this contrast?

To Kill a Mockingbird

Lee sets the novel in Maycomb – the setting mostly corresponds to the roaming range of the young Scout. It is centred on the Finch family home, with a fairly clear geography embracing the courthouse with its jail, the Negro church, the town dump and the schoolyard. The time period is the 1930s, and there are references to Hitler and Roosevelt.

The town's history is mentioned in Chapter 13, where its smallness and closed-in nature are emphasised – a town where Atticus believes 'nobody has much chance to be furtive'.

ACTIVITY 5
Settings in *To Kill a Mockingbird*

1. Why might Lee wish to emphasise the remoteness and closed-in nature of the little town?
2. Collect and note down some of the words and phrases used to describe the sleepy little town.

Animal Farm

The setting is the farm; the action never crosses its boundaries. Within the farm, memorable events take place in the barn, in the farmyard, on the knoll and, for the final scene in the novel, in the farmhouse itself.

ACTIVITY 6

Settings in Animal Farm

1. Discuss the following question in groups: Why do you think Orwell limits the setting in this way? He could, for example, have included scenes of Jones drinking in the Red Lion, or Frederick and Pilkington plotting on their farms, instead of just telling us about them. But he does not do so.
2. Write a paragraph suggesting reasons for his decision.

Of Mice and Men

There are four memorable settings:

- the pool on the Salinas River where the action begins and ends
- the bunkhouse
- Crooks's room
- the barn.

Review

Make sure you understand the settings of your novel and the effects the writer wishes to create — **atmosphere**, **contrast**, **character** and **action**.

ACTIVITY 7

Settings in Of Mice and Men

1. Collect the words and phrases Steinbeck uses to describe these settings.
2. What does the description of the bunkhouse tell us about the lives of the ranch workers?
3. What does the description of Crooks's room tell us about Crooks and his life? Look closely at the details here, as Steinbeck has chosen them very carefully.
4. Why do you think Steinbeck ends the book in the setting where it began? There is one difference: at the start there is a realistic description of rabbits sitting then hurrying for cover, but at the end there is a gigantic rabbit which 'waggled its ears' and talked to Lennie. Why do you think Steinbeck included this detail?

Unit 1 The Study of Prose

Plot 2

What is 'plot'?

The first interest of any reader coming to a new novel is probably the plot – in other words, what happens in the book.

The events that form a storyline are linked or connected with each other, from the beginning to the end. We call this linkage **structure**, or **plot structure**. Because the events are linked, they give us a satisfying and complete story.

In this section, we will look at some of the ways of linking material and then at how the writers of the six set texts go about this. You will find that discussing plot involves not only the 'linked series of events' in a novel, but also *why* writers shape their stories in the particular ways they do.

> **Key Word**
>
> **Plot**
> The linked sequence of events that forms the storyline

Sequence

Many novels follow a simple **chronological sequence** – the events of the story are described in the order in which they happen. Some novels – not all – use **flashback**. This is a scene set earlier than the main action. For example, in *Lord of the Flies*, when Ralph is struggling to cope with the worsening situation on the island, he allows his mind to drift back to happier days, when he was younger.

Climax

The writer will pay close attention to sequence. Events can be ordered so as to lead up to a **climax**. This happens with the mistakes Lennie makes in *Of Mice and Men*, which become more and more serious, ending in him killing the girl. Similarly, in *Lord of the Flies* the deaths among the boys become increasingly shocking to the reader.

> **Key Word**
>
> **Climax**
> The moment, usually at the end of the novel, when the writer makes their point most dramatically

Contrast

Events can also be sequenced so as to provide a deliberate **contrast**. For example, in *The Power and the Glory*, the reader is suddenly moved on from the desperation of the Priest, in danger of his life and sick with fever, to the comfort and security of life with the Lehrs. There is another example in *To Kill a Mockingbird*, where we move from the comedy of the Maycomb pageant (with Scout dressed ridiculously as a ham) to the near tragedy of the murder attempt on the children as they walk home.

11

Foreshadowing

Another way of linking material is by paralleling events in some way, so that one event seems to the reader to **foreshadow** another. There is a clear example in *Of Mice and Men*, where the shooting of Candy's dog (with the Luger pistol, in the back of the head) seems to foreshadow the shooting of Lennie, where the details are the same. As a result, the reader may start to wonder whether there are further similarities between the two events.

ACTIVITY 8

Considering plot structure

The following tasks focus on plot structure. Complete the tasks for the novel you have studied.

Things Fall Apart

Up to and including the killing of Ikemefuna, Achebe shows us that Okonkwo offends against the manners and customs of Umuofia on several occasions.

1 Describe what Okonkwo does to offend, and explain why he acts as he does.
2 Comment on the **sequence** of these 'offences'. What are our impressions of Okonkwo by this point in the novel?

Lord of the Flies

1 Look carefully at the description of Roger throwing stones at Henry in Chapter 4, which **foreshadows** his part in the killing of Piggy in Chapter 11. What explanation is Golding suggesting in Chapter 4 for Roger's actions in Chapter 11?

The Power and the Glory

In the last pages of Part 1 and in the last pages of Part 4, Greene gives two contrasting descriptions of encounters between Luis and the lieutenant.

1 Describe how Luis's behaviour changes.
2 Show **why** Greene makes this contrast.

To Kill a Mockingbird

When the children return home from First Purchase Church, they find Aunt Alexandra sitting on the porch.

1 Write a paragraph explaining why the events at the church and coming face to face with Aunt Alexandra is a particularly enjoyable **sequence of events** for the reader.
2 Explain why you think Lee has chosen to **juxtapose** (place close together) these events.

Animal Farm

In the novel, the Seven Commandments are altered.

1 List the **sequence of changes** made to the Seven Commandments painted on the wall of the barn.
2 Write a paragraph commenting on the changes made to the Seven Commandments.

The ~~Seven~~ Five Commandments of Animalism
~~Whatever goes upon two legs is an enemy.~~
~~Whatever goes upon four legs, or has wings, is a friend.~~
~~No animal shall wear clothes.~~
FOUR LEGS GOOD, TWO LEGS ~~BAD~~ BETTER
No animal shall sleep in a bed, with sheets.
No animal shall drink alcohol, to excess.
No animal shall kill any other animal, without cause.
All animals are equal, but some animals are more equal than others.

Of Mice and Men

In the second section of the novel, Steinbeck shows George interacting with most of the other characters.

1 List this sequence of encounters with short descriptions of each interaction.
2 Write a paragraph saying what you think Steinbeck's purpose was in this section.

Beginnings and endings

These are important to the structure of the plot. Obviously, the **beginning** of the novel is when the writer tries to engage the reader's attention and may give important first impressions of characters or setting.

ACTIVITY 9

Beginnings

In groups, discuss the following beginnings. (They may not be from your chosen novel, but can still be usefully discussed.)

1 Explore **how** the writer is trying to engage and interest the reader.
2 How successful do you find these openings? Give reasons for your opinions.

This opening is from *Animal Farm* by George Orwell.

> Mr Jones, of the Manor Farm, had locked the hen-houses for the night, but was too drunk to remember to shut the pop-holes. With the ring of light from his lantern dancing from side to side, he lurched across the yard, kicking off his boots at the back door, drew himself a last glass of beer from the barrel in the scullery, and made his way up to bed, where Mrs Jones was already snoring.
>
> As soon as the light in the bedroom went out there was a stirring and a fluttering all through the farm buildings. Word had gone round during the day that Old Major, the prize Middle White boar, had had a strange dream on the previous night and wished to communicate it to the other animals. It had been agreed that they should all meet in the big barn as soon as Mr Jones was safely out of the way. Old Major (so he was always called, though the name under which he had been exhibited was Willingdon Beauty) was so highly regarded on the farm that everyone was quite ready to lose an hour's sleep in order to hear what he had to say.

This opening is from *Things Fall Apart* by Chinua Achebe.

> Okonkwo was well known throughout the nine villages and even beyond. His fame rested on solid personal achievements. As a young man of eighteen he had brought honour to his village by throwing Amalinze the Cat. Amalinze was the great wrestler who for seven years was unbeaten, from Umuofia to Mbaino. He was called the Cat because his back would never touch the earth. It was this man that Okonkwo threw in a fight which the old men agreed was one of the fiercest since the founder of their town engaged a spirit of the wild for seven days and seven nights.
>
> The drums beat and the flutes sang and the spectators held their breath. Amalinze was a wily craftsman, but Okonkwo was as slippery as a fish in water. Every nerve and every muscle stood out on their arms, on their backs and their thighs, and one almost heard them stretching to breaking point. In the end Okonkwo threw the Cat.

A novel may **end** in a number of ways – with a climax, or in uncertainty, or with an invitation to the reader to reflect on what they have read.

ACTIVITY 10
Endings

Look at the ending of the novel you are studying. Write a paragraph about it in which you answer the following questions:

- Is the ending clearly linked to the previous events of the novel?
- Does it involve the major character or characters of the novel, or minor ones, or even new ones? Comment on this.
- Does it contain the climax of the novel – the most intense and interesting event in the plot?

Review

Let's review some of the key words and ideas used in this section:

- **plot**
- **contrast**
- **structure**
- **foreshadowing**
- **chronological sequence**
- **juxtaposition**
- **flashback**

Make sure you understand each term clearly. Make a list of definitions which you can use for revision.

Theme 3

What is a theme?

Writers have a clear purpose in writing a novel, other than producing 'a good read'. They may wish to raise awareness of particular topics, to make readers think about issues and perhaps even to change attitudes towards these issues. So, as we read, we gradually realise that there are ideas behind the story which the author is exploring; these are the themes. A novel may have more than one theme.

> **Key Word**
> **Themes**
> The main ideas explored in a novel

We have already looked at plot. It is important to understand the differences between the plot and the themes of a novel.

For example, *Animal Farm* tells the story of how the animals on a farm, angry because they have been mistreated, rebel against the farmer and set up their own farm, governing themselves. This is the **plot**, the linked series of events.	However, the writer, Orwell, is interested in certain issues which are communicated through the plot. For example, we could say that he is interested in revolutions, in how they succeed and how they fail. Or that he is interested in how those who gain power are corrupted by it. These more general issues are **themes**.
Similarly, *Lord of the Flies* tells the story of how a plane crashes on a tropical island and what happens to the boys who survive the crash.	But the writer, Golding, is interested in wider ideas, and uses this story to show us something about, for example, the theme of bullying, or the evil existing in human nature.

Writer's technique

In the examination, there will be a question which focuses on a theme in the novel you have studied. Here is an example of a **theme-focused** question on *Of Mice and Men*:

> With reference to the ways Steinbeck **presents** the ranch workers, show how far you would agree that their lives are **lonely**.

The question is asking you to focus on how the writer explores the theme of loneliness in the novel. We can identify themes in a novel through the development of **plot**, **character** and **setting**. In *Of Mice and Men*, we can identify loneliness as a theme because Steinbeck explores various forms of loneliness through:

- **Plot** – the story of George and Lennie's journey to the ranch and their time working there.
- **Character** – Steinbeck explores the theme of loneliness through the ways characters are described and behave towards each other.
- **Setting** – the descriptions of the ranch, especially the living conditions for the ranch workers, underline the theme of loneliness.

Workers in America during the 1930s

Therefore, when answering the theme-focused question, you could discuss each of these features of the novel to present an argument about how lonely the ranch workers are.

Similarly, masculinity is a theme in *Things Fall Apart* because Achebe explores ideas about masculinity through:

- **Plot** – the story of Okonkwo's life and death.
- **Character** – Okonkwo's actions and the similar or contrasting way other men in Umuofia behave.
- **Setting** – the village and clan of Umuofia having its own ideas about masculinity.

You can be sure that there will be a theme-focused question on your novel in the examination, so it makes sense to do some forward thinking about what themes there might be in that question.

ACTIVITY 11

Working with your chosen novel – the main themes

Completing a table like the one below should help you to form clear ideas about how the writer of your novel uses plot to convey their themes. (We will look at characters and setting in Activity 13.)

Theme	Key incident	Useful words and phrases

1. Copy the table above and write **two or three** main themes in your novel in the first column. (There are some suggestions on page 18 about themes in each novel.)
2. Think of a key incident or incidents from your novel where each theme you have identified is developed. **Briefly** describe these incidents in the second column.
3. Select useful words and phrases from the text as evidence to support your thoughts.

Don't go into too much detail in the second and third columns. It is more important to **select the key incidents** and the **most useful words and phrases**.

ACTIVITY 12

Reviewing themes in your novel – looking further

Draw a new table with the same headings as in Activity 11 but this time leave space to add two more columns on the right. (You will need the extra columns in Activity 13 on page 19.)

Look at each of the themes listed below from your chosen novel. Make notes under the three headings on the ways your author explores these themes through key incidents (plot) in their novel. This table will be very useful during your revision for the final examination.

Things Fall Apart
- Change and tradition
- Masculinity
- Different faiths
- Life in the village
- Family

Lord of the Flies
- Rules and behaviour
- Fear
- Rescue
- End of innocence
- The beast
- Civilisation versus savagery

The Power and the Glory
- Martyrdom
- Humility
- Idealism and realism
- Guilt
- Responsibility

To Kill a Mockingbird
- Learning about life/growing up
- Prejudice
- Unfairness
- Family life
- Courage

Animal Farm
- Equality
- Power
- Exploitation
- Life on the farm

Of Mice and Men
- Life on the ranch
- Friendship
- Plans for the future/dreams
- Loneliness
- Power
- Conflict

We have considered how writers use the **plot** to develop key themes in their novels. Writers also use **setting** and **character** to elaborate their themes. For example, in *To Kill a Mockingbird*, Lee explores the theme of prejudice through the setting of the town of Maycomb. The descriptions of Maycomb and its rigid social divisions add to the reader's understanding of the prejudice which Lee calls 'Maycomb's usual disease'.

> **Examiner's tip!**
> Be aware of the wording of the question! For example, a question on *To Kill a Mockingbird* may ask about how Scout 'matures' rather than how she 'learns lessons about life' or 'grows up'.

Greene fleshes out his theme of guilt in *The Power and the Glory* through the character of the Priest and his interactions with the villagers as he tries to avoid being caught by the Lieutenant and his men. The descriptions of the Priest at various points in the novel help us to understand how guilt has affected his life and the choices he makes. It is in ways like these that writers explore the issues which they want to address in their novels.

ACTIVITY 13

Linking themes with characters and settings

1. Look back at the table you created in Activity 12 on page 17 and add two columns headed 'Characters' and 'Settings'.
2. For each theme you have identified, list relevant characters and settings which are used to develop the theme. These notes should be brief but informative enough to help your revision.

ACTIVITY 14

Developing your ideas

This activity is intended to help you to develop the work you did in Activities 11–13, and should help you firm up your thinking on themes in your chosen novel.

Write an extended paragraph on **one** of the themes in your novel. Consider the following points in planning your response:

- Which **characters** are particularly important for understanding this theme?
- What **incidents** are particularly important and why?
- Is the **setting** of the novel relevant to understanding what the writer is saying about this theme? If it is, explain in what ways it is important.

Use brief quotations to illustrate the points you make.

You should repeat this activity for each of the important themes in your chosen novel.

Review

Remember, there will be a **theme-focused** question as one of your choices on the examination so it is important to understand the themes in the novel you have studied and the ways the writer has explored each theme. When planning your answer, think about the tables you have created in this section and how the writer explores the theme identified in the question through **plot**, **character** and **setting**.

Character 4

What is 'character'?

Discussing characters in a novel involves more than a simple physical description or 'character study'. What you will need to examine is **characterisation**, or the process by which the writer reveals the personality of a character.

This means you must remember that characters are deliberately created by the writer. As readers, we need to be aware of the ways writers create and develop characters for us.

There will be a question in the examination which focuses on **character**. At (H) tier, this question will usually start with the words:

> With reference to the ways the author **presents** [the named character] . . .

The key word here is **presents**. This word is in the question to encourage you to focus on the **techniques** the writer uses to create character.

Writer's technique

Explicit descriptions

Characters can be revealed directly through the writer's descriptions. For example, Steinbeck's description of Lennie in *Of Mice and Men* gives the reader a clear impression of his appearance.

Look at the underlined words in this description. What impression is Steinbeck trying to create?

> Behind him walked his opposite, a huge man, shapeless of face, with large, pale eyes, with wide, sloping shoulders; and he walked heavily, dragging his feet a little, the way a bear drags its paws.

Key Word

Characterisation
The ways a writer conveys information to help the reader form an impression of a character

Examiner's tip!

Focus on the writer's technique in your answer by discussing the use of **words and phrases** and the use of **imagery**, as well as the impressions you form of the characters. The discussion of writer's technique is one of the secrets of success in this examination!

Lennie

Such a description influences our attitudes towards a character. Steinbeck helps the reader picture Lennie, especially through linking him with animals. The start of the description clearly describes Lennie's size; he is a 'huge man . . . with wide, sloping shoulders'.

However, you can move past the obvious description to develop a fuller picture of Lennie. The use of words such as 'heavily' and 'dragging his feet' gives the impression of someone moving clumsily, shuffling along. This description is highlighted by the comparison to a bear, emphasising Lennie's shape and stature and adding to our sense of him being slow and awkward.

Key Word

Direct characterisation
Explicit information used to build an impression of a character

ACTIVITY 15
Direct characterisation

1. Focus on **one** character from your chosen novel. Consider the way this character's appearance is described.
2. Create a table like the one below identifying how the character is described and the impressions these descriptions form.

Description	This tells me . . .

Key Word

Indirect characterisation
The implicit methods a writer uses to develop an impression of a character

Writers also develop characterisation **indirectly** through a range of methods.

Speech

- What does the character say?
- How does the character speak? Think of use of dialect or tone.

Look at this extract from *Things Fall Apart*.

> '*Tufia-a!*' the priestess cursed, her voice cracking like the angry bark of thunder in the dry season. 'How dare you, woman, to go before the mighty Agbala of your own accord! Beware, woman, lest he strike you in his anger. Bring me my daughter.'

The description of the way the priestess speaks gives us an idea of her character. She is angry and demanding, but is also in a position of power which is shown by her warnings and commands – 'Beware' and 'Bring me my daughter'.

Thoughts

- What information can we take from a description of the character's thoughts and feelings?

In *To Kill a Mockingbird*, we learn a lot about Scout from her thoughts. For example in Chapter 24, we can see how Scout's attitude towards Aunt Alexandra is changing, showing that Scout is becoming more mature.

> Aunt Alexandra looked across the room at me and smiled . . . I carefully picked up the tray and watched myself walk to Mrs Merriweather. With my very best company manners, I asked her if she would like some. After all, if Aunty could be a lady at a time like this, so could I.

Actions

- What does the character do? How does the character behave?

Look at this extract from *Animal Farm*. What do we learn about Snowball's character from his actions in this incident?

> Snowball now gave the signal for the charge. He himself dashed straight for Jones. Jones saw him coming, raised his gun and fired. The pellets scored bloody streaks along Snowball's back, and a sheep dropped dead. Without halting for an instant Snowball flung his fifteen stone against Jones's legs.

Snowball appears heroic and in command in this description. He leads the charge and, even when wounded, fights on 'without halting for an instant'.

Interactions with others

- What do we learn about a character from the way they interact with others?
- How do others behave in reaction to the character?
- What do others say about the character?

In *The Power and the Glory*, we can learn a lot about the character of the Priest through his interactions with his daughter. His love and guilt are clearly demonstrated.

> He saw her fixed in her life like a fly in amber. . . . He prayed silently, 'O God, give me any kind of death – without contrition, in a state of sin – only save this child.'
> He was a man who was supposed to save souls.

Contrast

- Does the writer deliberately contrast characters to create impressions for the reader?

For example, in *Lord of the Flies*, Golding creates a contrast between Ralph and Roger through his initial descriptions of each character.

> The boy with the fair hair . . . You could see now that he might make a boxer, as far as width and heaviness of shoulders went, but there was a mildness about his mouth and eyes that proclaimed no devil.

> There was a slight, furtive boy whom no one knew, who kept to himself with an inner intensity of avoidance and secrecy . . . The dark boy, Roger . . .

These two descriptions from Chapter 1 establish the reader's first impressions of these characters by highlighting the explicit contrast between 'fair' and 'dark'. The differences are reinforced by the descriptions of Ralph's 'mildness about his mouth and eyes', and Roger as 'furtive' and withdrawn, conveying contrasting characteristics of openness and secretiveness.

ACTIVITY 16

Indirect characterisation

In this activity, focus on the character from your chosen novel listed below:

- Obierika in *Things Fall Apart*
- Jack in *Lord of the Flies*
- The Priest in *The Power and the Glory*
- Scout in *To Kill a Mockingbird*
- Squealer in *Animal Farm*
- George in *Of Mice and Men*

1 Create a concept map of all your impressions of this character. Aim for six to eight points about them.

2 Take each point from your concept map and identify in simple bullet points the techniques the writer uses to create these impressions.

Remember to give evidence from the text to support your comments.

Think about how the writer uses methods of characterisation such as **explicit descriptions, speech, thoughts, actions, interactions with others and contrasts**.

3 Write up your notes about the character in paragraphs.

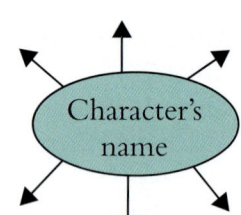

Examiner's tip!

Writers will not use every method covered in this section in every novel. For example, we can form a clear picture of Snowball from *Animal Farm* through what he says, his actions, his interactions and the contrast between him and Napoleon – but we never read his thoughts.

Examiner's tip!

Sometimes the question will ask you to give **your** opinion of a character – this is to encourage you to give your personal response to the text. Think carefully about the character and your reaction to them. Remember to explain **why** you react to the character in a particular way.

Review

Remember that when you are discussing characters in a novel you must:

- show knowledge of who the character is and what the character does
- examine **how** the writer develops the character.

Language and style 5

In the examination you will be asked to consider the language, style and structure of your chosen novel. This is shown by the key term **presents** in the question. If you discuss the writer's technique, your answer is likely to excel.

Features to consider are the writer's use of language, narrative point of view, dialogue and structure.

Writer's technique

Use of language

The writer's use of imagery, especially **similes** and **metaphors**, may be revealing.

For example, the comparison in *Of Mice and Men* of how Lennie 'walked heavily, dragging his feet a little, the way a bear drags his paws' suggests both Lennie's strength and his clumsiness. So the simile is used as a method of characterisation.

In this passage from *To Kill a Mockingbird*, Bob Ewell takes the witness stand.

> . . . a little bantam cock of a man rose and strutted to the stand, the back of his neck reddening at the sound of his name. When he turned around to take the oath, we saw that his face was as red as his neck. We also saw no resemblance to his namesake. A shock of wispy new-washed hair stood up from his forehead; his nose was thin, pointed and shiny; he had no chin to speak of – it seemed to be a part of his crepey neck.
> ' – so help me God', he crowed.

Narrative point of view

The story will be shaped by the narrator. It may have an omniscient narrator (who knows everything, including the characters' thoughts and feelings): for example, the narrator in *Lord of the Flies*, through whom we enter into the mind of the central character, Ralph.

The story may be told through the eyes of one of the characters – who may not know everything. *To Kill a Mockingbird* is an interesting example. The main narrator is a young girl, Scout, who neither knows nor fully understands all that is going on. So, at times, readers may feel that they know more than the narrator.

Dialogue

Dialogue is direct speech between characters, and may convey their thoughts and feelings. It allows the writer to comment less directly on the characters and lets them reveal themselves.

ACTIVITY 17

Use of metaphor

In the extended metaphor in the extract on the right, Harper Lee compares Bob Ewell to a 'bantam cock'.

1. List all the words and phrases that continue this metaphor.
2. Write a paragraph to suggest reasons why Lee makes this comparison.

Use of symbols

This can be a method of expressing meaning in few words by using an object which has some significance in the telling of the story: for example, the conch in *Lord of the Flies*, the mockingbird in *To Kill a Mockingbird*, or the locusts in *Things Fall Apart*. Using a symbol has a second advantage for a writer: the meaning does not have to be spelt out, but can be suggested indirectly.

Language and style in your chosen novel

These activities and the accompanying information encourage you to think about how language is used in each text. Complete the tasks for your chosen novel.

Things Fall Apart

> **ACTIVITY 19**
>
> **Language in *Things Fall Apart***
>
> Many Ibo words are used in the novel. Some of them are translated; some of them are not. If they are translated, we don't need the Ibo words, and if they are not translated we may not understand the full meaning.
>
> 1 What is the point of using the Ibo words?
>
> 2 Frequent use is made in the novel of folk tales, songs and verses. Collect some of these and write a short paragraph explaining what they tell us of the way of life in Umuofia.

> **ACTIVITY 18**
>
> **Dialogue in *Things Fall Apart***
>
> The dialogue between men in this novel is sometimes very formal. For example, Okoye's conversation with Unoka in Chapter 1 is very polite and conducted partly in proverbs.
>
> 1 What impressions do you get of the men of the clan from this and similar pieces of dialogue? Find other examples of the use of proverbs in the dialogue of the novel.
>
> 2 What is the writer's intention here? The language used in dialogue is far from colloquial English:
>
> > 'Is it true that Okonkwo nearly killed you with his gun?'
> > 'It is true indeed, my dear friend, I cannot yet find a mouth with which to tell the story.'

Lord of the Flies

Golding mixes and **contrasts** passages of description with rapid dialogue.

At times, he describes nature so that it seems to echo the mood of the boys. This is called **pathetic fallacy**. For example, the description of the sunset and oncoming darkness (end of Chapter 2) is linked to the boys' fear as they realise what they have done with their 'small fire'.

A memorable passage is the description of the storm which accompanies the killing of Simon. This is described in striking figurative language ('the white and brown clouds brooded . . . the dark sky was shattered by a blue–white scar . . . a great wind blew the rain sideways, cascading the water from the forest trees . . .').

> **Key Word**
>
> **Pathetic fallacy**
> Attributing human feelings to nature

ACTIVITY 21

Dialogue in *Lord of the Flies*

Despite the reference to the 'many brilliant speeches' made at the assemblies, there are almost no long speeches in the novel. Look at the dialogue at the end of Chapter 6, beginning 'We want smoke. And you go wasting your time. You roll rocks . . .', and ending with 'Are you all off your rockers?' In groups, discuss:

1 What is most noticeable about this conversation?
2 Which boys in the novel would you expect to make long speeches? What happens when they try to do so, and what are they trying to speak about?

ACTIVITY 20

Description in *Lord of the Flies*

1 Read the account of Simon's death, noting down vivid and memorable words and phrases used to describe the storm. The example on page 25 will give you a start.
2 Write a brief explanation of why Golding describes the storm rather than concentrating on narrating the shocking event of Simon's death.

The Power and the Glory

ACTIVITY 22

Imagery in *The Power and the Glory*

What is the significance of these images?

- The snake-like fangs of the mestizo
- The ever-present vultures
- The Priest struggling with the bitch for a bone

ACTIVITY 24

Contrast in *The Power and the Glory*

Keeping in mind the point in Activity 23 about opposites existing together, read the description of the Lieutenant halfway through Part 1 Chapter 2 beginning 'The Lieutenant walked home through the shuttered town . . .' and ending three paragraphs later with 'He was a mystic, too, and what he had experienced was vacancy – a complete certainty in the existence of a dying, cooling world, of human beings who had evolved from animals for no purpose at all. He knew.'

1 List the words and phrases here that link the Lieutenant with the religion he so despises. What is the writer's intention in using such imagery?
2 Write a number of paragraphs comparing and contrasting the Priest and the Lieutenant. Use the points below to help you.
   - Both men are described as looking like a 'black question mark'.
   - The Priest says to the Lieutenant, 'You're a good man'; the Lieutenant says to the Priest, 'You aren't a bad fellow'.
   - Both love children and wish to protect them.
   - Both hate poverty.
   - Physical contrast between the two men.

ACTIVITY 23

Symbols in *The Power and the Glory*

Alcohol is necessary for the Priest to carry out his sacred duty. However, he feels that alcohol is part of his ruination. Ironically, the brandy mentioned is 'Vera Cruz' (true cross)! Like much else in the novel, alcohol seems to be two sided, to have both a positive and a negative meaning.

How does this two-sidedness apply to the mestizo and the Fellows family?

ACTIVITY 26

Contrast in *To Kill a Mockingbird*

1. Contrast Jem's 'reasonable description' of Boo Radley in Chapter 1 with his tears at the verdict at the beginning of Chapter 22.
2. What does each of these tell the reader about his view of the world?

Key Word

Structure
The way the parts of a novel are connected together

ACTIVITY 25

Language in *The Power and the Glory*

Discuss in groups:

1. Why are three of the most important characters in the novel unnamed?
2. The mestizo is referred to as Judas. What other biblical references can you find in the novel?

To Kill a Mockingbird

To Kill a Mockingbird is divided into two parts which reflect the interests and attitudes of Scout – but more especially of Jem. He is always more mature than Scout, but in Part 1 his interests are still childish – for example the Boo Radley game. At the end of Part 1, Jem has two important experiences (seeing his father shoot the mad dog, and reading to Mrs Dubose) which prepare him for what is to happen in Part 2, when he watches the trial and learns about the racism of his home town. So the **structure** of the novel helps to convey the theme of growing up.

ACTIVITY 27

Characterisation through speech in *To Kill a Mockingbird*

How characters speak is often used in novels as a method of **characterisation**. The differences in speech add interest and variety.

Here are two passages where Lee characterises the speaker through the way they speak.

> 'I got somethin' to say an' then I ain't gonna say no more. That nigger yonder took advantage of me, an' if you fine fancy gentlemen don't wanta do nothin' about it then you're all yellow stinkin' cowards, the lot of you. Your fancy airs don't come to nothin' – your ma'amin' and Miss Mayellerin' don't come to nothing, Mr Finch.' (Mayella Ewell)

> 'Gertrude, I tell you there's nothing more distracting than a sulky darky. Their mouths go down to here. Just ruins your day to have one of 'em in the kitchen. You know what I said to my Sophy, Gertrude? I said, "Sophy" I said, "you simply are not being a Christian today. Jesus Christ never went around grumbling and complaining." And you know it did her good. She took her eyes off that floor and said "Nome, Miz Merriweather, Jesus never went around grumblin'." I tell you, Gertrude, you never ought to let an opportunity go by to witness for the Lord.' (Mrs Merriweather – at the missionary tea)

1. Make notes on the way these characters speak. Back up the points you make about each with carefully chosen examples.
2. Do the same for Atticus, using some of his speeches in court.

Animal Farm

Orwell believed in 'using the fewest and shortest words that will cover one's meaning', and usually in *Animal Farm* the narrator tells the story in a simple style.

When Orwell breaks this 'rule' there is usually a reason. Look at Snowball's explanation to the birds that 'a bird's wing . . . is an organ of propulsion and not an organ of manipulation. It should therefore be regarded as a leg. The distinguishing mark of Man is the *hand*, the instrument with which he does all his mischief . . .' (Chapter 3). The narrator tells us that the birds did not understand Snowball's 'long words', but Orwell uses them because he wishes to show Snowball expressing some of the political theory of Animalism.

ACTIVITY 28
Language in *Animal Farm*

Squealer uses various kinds of language: slogans, threats, simple language and 'long words'.

Find examples of each of these four types of language being used by Squealer and write a short explanation of why Squealer uses them.

ACTIVITY 29
Rhetorical devices in *Animal Farm*

The longest speech in *Animal Farm* is that of Old Major in Chapter 1. In it he uses many rhetorical tricks and devices.

Working in groups, find an example of each of the following rhetorical techniques in Old Major's speech. Write a paragraph explaining why Old Major uses them.

- Repetition of words, phrases and sentence patterns
- Direct address to the audience
- Rhetorical questions
- Vivid phrases
- Prophesying the future
- Exclamation
- Compression of message into one word
- Black-and-white view of things

Review

Let's review some of the key words and ideas used in this section:

- **imagery**
- **dialogue**
- **narrator**
- **symbol.**

Make sure you understand each term clearly. Make a list of definitions which you can use for revision.

Of Mice and Men

As we read a novel, we may notice that a scene or action is repeated – though not perhaps in exactly the same form. So we can compare *and* contrast, finding similarities and differences.

This **structure** gives us an interesting way to look at *Of Mice and Men*.

ACTIVITY 30
Structure of *Of Mice and Men*

1 Look at the instances where George tells Lennie about the happy life they will have on their farm. Make notes on **how many times** the story is told, and **why** George tells it on each occasion.

2 Review your notes and point out what remains the same and what changes in George's descriptions.

3 Make notes on the 'bad things' which Lennie does. What similarities are there? Is there a pattern to what happens?

4 Examine George's reactions to Lennie's bad behaviour in Chapters 1 and 6. Select the words that show the differences between George's reactions on these two occasions.

5 Suggest reasons why George's reactions to Lennie's behaviour change.

Language and style

27

6 Bringing it all together

Some reminders about the Prose unit (Unit 1)

What is being assessed?
- Your knowledge and understanding of the novel; your ability to develop an argument about it.
- Your understanding of the writer's technique.
- 'Quality of written communication'.

Time and planning
The examination for the Prose unit (Unit 1) lasts **1 hour**. You answer **one** question. You can choose to answer either a **theme-focused** or a **character-focused** question on the novel you have studied.

It is most important that you **plan** your answer, especially at Higher tier, where there are no guiding bullet points. Beforehand, in class, you should discuss and practise how to manage the 60 minutes for both extract-based and free-standing questions. Without planning, your answer is likely to be incoherent, so do not be too impatient to get started. Remember that 'Quality of written communication' is assessed in this examination. You have more time for this question than for any other question in the examination.

Regulations
This is a 'closed-book' examination, which means you may *not* bring a copy of the novel into the examination. A Resource Booklet will be provided for use in answering the extract-based question.

How many marks?

The Prose unit (Unit 1) is worth 25 per cent of the available marks towards your final English Literature grade.

'Quality of written communication'
This is assessed in all units of the examination. You should take care to:

- choose an appropriate form and style for your answer

- organise your material clearly and coherently (e.g. taking care with punctuation and paragraphing)
- write legibly and accurately.

' **The use of quotation**

This is probably less worrying than you think. This is a closed-book examination, and the examiner will be realistic. However, here are some useful tips:

- Quotation is certainly one way of demonstrating your knowledge of the text, but it is not the only way! **Accurate** and **well-selected** reference to the text can help develop your argument and support your ideas.
- Use quotations to make, illustrate or back up a point. Don't waste time by using them to repeat a point, or simply because you have learnt them!
- Try to make your quotations accurate – though here again the examiner will be realistic.
- Present quotations in inverted commas.
- If the quotation cannot stand alone, make it fit into the surrounding sentence.
- Quotations should be **brief**, **meaningful** and **relevant**. '

Question types

Extract-based questions

The **extract-based** questions considered here are **(a)** questions.

Foundation tier and Higher tier questions

The questions at Foundation tier have bullet points to help you structure your argument. Here are examples of a Foundation tier question and a Higher tier question (on *Lord of the Flies*) for comparison.

In the examination, the extract referred to would be printed in the Resource Booklet. Extract 2 can be found on the CCEA website (GCSE English Literature Specimen Assessment Materials): www.ccea.org.uk

> **F** (a) With reference to extract 2 and elsewhere in the novel, show how Simon is **different** from the other boys.
>
> In your answer you should consider the **presentation** of:
>
> - his actions and behaviour in the extract
> - Simon's behaviour in the rest of the novel
> - the things that Simon comes to understand about the beast.

> **H** (a) With reference to the ways Golding **presents** Simon in extract 2 and elsewhere in the novel, show how far you would agree that Simon is **different** from the other boys.

Bringing it all together

> **Examiner's tip!**
>
> Remember – you are not being asked to write everything you know about the character! Your answer **must focus** on the key terms of the question.

Unpacking the questions

Both of the questions on page 29 use some key terms which are there to guide you and help you to focus your ideas. These terms are in bold to bring them to your attention:

- **different** helps you to organise the material and focus your argument
- **presentation** or **presents** reminds you that you must deal with the writer's intentions and techniques.

You may have noted that there is a slight difference in the instruction words. At Foundation tier the question asks you to 'show how', so you will be demonstrating in what ways Simon is different from the others. However, at Higher tier the instruction 'show how far you would agree that' asks you to go a bit further. You may be agreeing, disagreeing, or partly agreeing that Simon is different. At both Foundation tier and Higher tier the word 'show' means that you must provide **evidence** for your opinions.

At Foundation tier, the bullet points suggest not only the areas of the novel to look at, but also a helpful order in which to consider them. This gives you a little extra support in constructing an argument in response to the question. At Higher tier, you are expected to build an argument based on the key terms of the question. This is why it is so important to spend some time planning your answer before making a start.

Although you have a printed extract to work from, it is important to remember that **both** the extract and the novel as a whole must be considered.

Free-standing essay questions

Foundation tier and Higher tier questions

Now let's look at a pair of free-standing essay questions (on *Lord of the Flies*). Note that the free-standing essay questions considered here are **(b)** questions, though you may get a free-standing essay question as either **(a)** or **(b)**. The questions at Foundation tier have bullet points to help you structure your argument.

> (b) Show how rescue **becomes less important** to the boys as the novel progresses.
>
> In your answer you should consider the **presentation** of:
>
> - the signal fire
> - what Ralph says about rescue
> - the behaviour of Jack and the hunters.

> (b) With reference to the ways Golding **presents** characters and events in the novel, show how far you would agree that rescue **becomes less important** to the boys as the novel progresses.

Unpacking the questions

Once again each question has two key terms:

- **becomes less important** helps you to organise the material and focus your argument
- **presentation** or **presents** reminds you that you must deal with the writer's intentions and techniques.

Again, there is a slight difference in the instruction words. At Foundation tier, the words 'show how' mean you will be demonstrating in what ways rescue becomes less important to the boys. At Higher tier, the words 'show how far you would agree that' ask you to consider a counter argument in that you may be agreeing, disagreeing, or partly agreeing that rescue becomes less important to the boys. At both Foundation tier and Higher tier the word 'show' means that you must provide evidence for your opinions.

As with the **(a)** question, at Foundation tier the bullet points suggest not only the areas of the novel to look at, but also a helpful order in which to consider them. At Higher tier, you are given more freedom as it is up to you to select which references to the text will help you to construct your argument. As you do not have an extract to work from, planning is even more important here. Jot down points which are relevant, then sort these points into a coherent order which you can then develop in your answer. Avoid writing a very general essay – to 'score big' you have to focus on the key terms.

How your work is marked

The examiner will be looking for certain key features in your answer:

- **Focus** – Has your response answered the question?
- **Development** – Have you gone into detail?
- **Argument** – Is your response logical and persuasive?
- **Understanding** – Does it show understanding of use of language, characters, events and settings?

These are what you must produce in your answer to ensure success.

Assessment Objectives (AOs)

In this Prose unit (Unit 1), you need to cover the following two AOs and demonstrate that you can:

✓ **AO1** Respond to texts critically and imaginatively; select and evaluate relevant textual detail to illustrate and support interpretations.

✓ **AO2** Explain how language, structure and form contribute to writers' presentation of ideas, themes and settings.

Things Fall Apart by Chinua Achebe

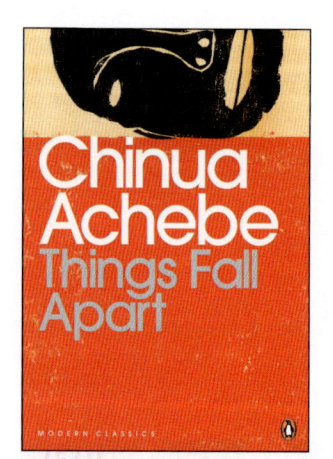

You will find both the extract and Mark Schemes for these questions on the CCEA website (www.ccea.org.uk)

Let's apply your skills to a free-standing essay question.

> **H** With reference to the ways Achebe **presents** Ikemefuna's life and death, show how far you would agree that he is a **pitiable** character.

A Band 2 response will be basic and straightforward, for example:

*Tries to **focus** on key term.*

Describes what happens.

> Ikemefuna is pitiable because he had to leave his own village and live in Umuofia. This meant he had to leave his mother and sister and live with strangers like Okonkwo so he is afraid.
>
> Ikemefuna lives with Okonkwo and his family and does chores. But he is not really part of the family and the elders decide that he has to be killed.

***Awareness** of character.*

Think carefully! What could you do to answer this question more successfully? For example:

- Move away from simple description and develop ideas with more discussion of the key term **pitiable**.
- Consider **how** the writer develops the character.
- Include **comments** about character and events rather than basic narrative.

Consider this sample Band 4 response:

*Some **interpretation** of character.*

> Ikemefuna can be considered pitiable mainly because of the reasons for him coming to Umuofia. He was separated from his mother and sister and sent to live among strangers in Umuofia as part of compensation for the death of a village girl. He is unaware of these reasons, which makes him pitiable as he doesn't understand what is going on, this change must be very confusing for him.
>
> However, when he settles into life in Umuofia, he is described as adapting well, becoming almost like an older brother to Okonkwo's son, Nwoye. We can see that he is happy in his new life when we read that his old home becomes a distant memory and even Okonkwo seems to be fond of him. So, although he appeared pitiable when he was taken from his home, his new circumstances seem to be quite pleasant.

***Sustains** focus on **pitiable**.*

This response is more developed and the student presents an argument based on the key term **pitiable**. A well planned answer will produce a coherent argument.

> **ACTIVITY 31**
>
> **Answering a free-standing essay question**
> 1. Look again at the Band 4 response above. How could you develop it? Write some bullet points.
> 2. Now, go ahead and answer the question!

Examiner's tip!

Bring the writer into it. If you want to produce a good answer, you must deal with how he presents the material. Remember to use the key term **pitiable**.

Now, let's look at an extract-based question.

> H With reference to the ways Achebe **presents** the white missionaries in the extract and elsewhere in the novel, show how far you would agree that they bring **destruction** to Umuofia's way of life.

Examiner's tip!

The extract is there to encourage you to address writer's technique. Use it!

Here is part of a Band 3 response:

> The passage makes it clear that the white men have brought destruction to Umuofia. The first paragraph hints at the violence associated with the white missionaries – the men of Umuofia feel that they have to go 'about armed with a gun or a matchet'. This sense of foreboding seems to be lifted when the men meet with the commissioner who speaks 'cordially' and appears to show understanding – 'my men . . . are ignorant of your customs.' However this soon changes when the men of Umuofia are ambushed. The description of their treatment gives the impression that the white men do not respect them and their way of life, hinting at the destruction to come.

- Uses quotation correctly.
- Comments on writer's technique.
- Focuses on **destruction**.

This student focuses on the key term **destruction** and shows understanding of the writer's technique.

⚠ Think carefully! What could you do to answer this question more fully? For example:

- Consider the words 'show how far' – do the white missionaries bring only destruction to Umuofia?
- Examine the extract in detail – look at the writer's use of language in the extract, for example, the words used to describe the humiliated emissaries from Umuofia. What **effect** is Achebe trying to create?
- What other incidents in the novel are relevant? Consider the massacre at Abame.

ACTIVITY 32

Answering an extract-based question
1. Look carefully at the extract and the sample response.
2. Use the points on the left to answer the question in full.

Bringing it all together

33

Lord of the Flies by William Golding

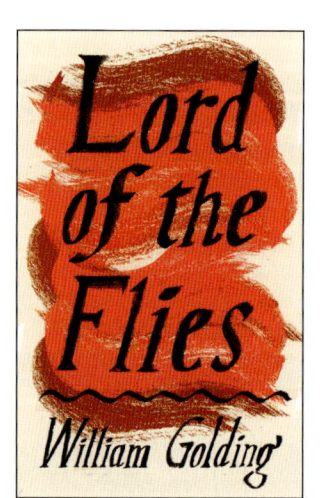

You will find both the extract and Mark Schemes for these questions on the CCEA website (www.ccea.org.uk).

Let's apply your skills to an extract-based question.

> **H** With reference to the ways Golding **presents** Simon in the extract and elsewhere in the novel, show how far you agree that Simon is **different** from the other boys.

Here is part of a Band 3 response:

This response is *beginning* to consider the question and comment on the words the writer uses. How can it be improved?

> Simon is different to the other boys in a range of ways. He separates himself from the other boys, for example he goes off on his own to explore the island rather than joining the rest at the bathing pool. It says 'he turned his back' and 'Simon turned away from them' which clearly shows that he wanted to be apart from the rest of the boys.

Annotations: Begins to focus on question. Some understanding of use of language. Some comment on character.

Examiner's tip!
Use the extract. It gives you the opportunity to analyse the writer's use of language.

Think carefully! What could you do to answer this question more successfully? For example:

- Develop ideas – extend this discussion of how Simon isolates himself.
- Discuss the extract in **detail** – consider the description of Simon's exploration of the forest and his reactions.

Here is part of a Band 4 response:

> In this extract Simon's 'difference' is evident. He deliberately separates himself from the group and, although he starts off joining in with the others – 'he followed them', it is not long before he decides to go off on his own 'he turned his back on this'. Golding repeats this action later in the extract 'Simon turned away from them' letting the reader understand Simon's wish to be alone. Simon doesn't seem to worry about being alone or the way the others might react to him and seems happy when he finds a hiding place. However, Golding lets us know that he has some similarities with the others 'his feet were bare like Jack's'.

Annotations: Focus on key term. Uses quotation correctly. Interprets character. Comments on writer's technique.

This response is more developed and the student avoids simply describing what happens in the extract.

ACTIVITY 33
Answering an extract-based question

1. How would you complete the Band 4 response? Note down some bullet points.
2. Now, go ahead and answer the question.

Now, let's consider a free-standing essay question.

> **H** With reference to the ways Golding **presents** characters and events in the novel, show how far you agree that rescue **becomes less important** to the boys as the novel progresses.

Here is part of a Band 2 response:

Attempts to focus on question.

Narrative and descriptive – just retells story!

> At the start of the book the boys make a fire because they think that it will help them be rescued but they let the fire out. The fire is on the mountain and it sets fire to the forest and a boy is killed. Ralph is the only one who is bothered about the fire because the other boys want to go out and hunt.

Some awareness of character but not explicitly linked to focus of question.

This is a **basic** response which tries to retell the story but doesn't comment on the events or characters.

⚠ Think carefully! What could you do to answer this question more fully? For example:

- Focus on the key terms of the question (importance of rescue), rather than describing the fire.
- What other aspects of rescue are mentioned in the novel? Think about Ralph's continuous talk of rescue and Jack's obsession with hunting.

Here is part of a Band 4 response:

Interprets character.

> Ralph represents the need for rescue in the novel. He reassures Piggy, and possibly himself, that 'sooner or later a ship will put in here' and constantly refers to rescue in the assembly meetings, trying to make the other boys understand how important it is. Golding presents Ralph's need for rescue in his obsession with the signal fire and his reaction to the fire going out. He speaks 'furiously' and is angry that the others can't understand the importance of a signal.
>
> Ralph's obsession is contrasted with Jack's passion for hunting.
> ...

Sustained focus on rescue.

Some discussion of writer's technique.

ACTIVITY 34

Answering a free-standing essay question

1. Complete the second paragraph in the Band 4 response by contrasting Ralph and Jack's attitudes.
2. Now, go ahead and answer the question.

Examiner's tip!

Bring the writer into it. Discuss **how** Golding shows that rescue becomes less important.

The Power and the Glory by Graham Greene

You will find both the extract and Mark Schemes for these questions on the CCEA website (www.ccea.org.uk).

Let's apply your skills to an extract-based question.

> **H** With reference to the ways Greene **presents** the mestizo in the extract and elsewhere in the novel, show how far you agree that the mestizo is **unreliable**.

Here is part of a Band 2 response:

*Attempts to focus on **unreliable**.*

Aware of character.

Describes without making comments.

> The mestizo in the extract says he is a 'good Christian' but the Priest does not trust him. He tells lies and can't remember them so this gets him mixed up. I think he is unreliable. Later on he wants to turn the Priest in to the police so that he can make some money.

This response is basically a description of what happens, making some points but not developing them.

⚠ Think carefully! What could you do to answer this question more successfully? Consider these points:

- How do we know that the Priest does not trust the mestizo?
- Discuss the extract in detail – examine the way Greene describes the mestizo. What **effect** is he trying to create?

Look at this extract from a Band 4 response:

Uses quotation correctly.

Discusses effects of writer's technique.

Comments meaningfully on writer's technique.

> Greene presents the mestizo in a negative way, describing him as someone you would think of as being unreliable and untrustworthy. 'He said accusingly' shows us that he knows he is doing something wrong and goes on the attack. Even his physical appearance shows that he is not someone you can trust 'the two yellow canine teeth, the finger-nails scratching in the armpit' – this creates an image of someone dirty and disgusting.
>
> The most obvious example of how Greene presents the mestizo as being unreliable is at the end of the extract – 'He was in the presence of Judas.'

Sustained focus on key term.

This response is more developed and the student explicitly examines Greene's use of language, making comments on the effects of the language. Look at the second paragraph in particular.

ACTIVITY 35

Answering an extract-based question

1. Look again at the second paragraph in the Band 4 response and develop this point in more detail by analysing the significance of the reference to Judas. How would you complete this response? Note down some bullet points.
2. Consider **how** the mestizo is presented elsewhere in the novel. Note down some bullet points.
3. Now, go ahead and answer the question.

Examiner's tip!
Use the extract. It gives you the opportunity to analyse the writer's use of language.

Now, let's consider a free-standing essay question.

> With reference to the ways Greene **presents** the characters in the novel, show to what extent contact with the Priest **changes** their behaviour.

Examiner's tip!
Bring the writer into it. Discuss **how** Greene describes the ways characters **react** to the Priest.

Here is part of a Band 3 response:

[Focuses on key terms of question.]
[Shows understanding of use of language.]
[Comments on events.]

> We can see that the Priest changes the behaviour and attitude of the Lieutenant. He is a man who believes completely in his work for the Revolution. He is described as hating churchmen and is called 'a dapper figure of hate'. However, when he comes into contact with the Priest, he does show a change in attitude. He treats the Priest quite well and is surprised that the Priest is so humble, as it goes against what he has been led to believe. Though he carries out the execution, he does it with a single shot to minimise the Priest's pain. I think there is some change in his attitude even though it is reluctant.

This student considers the key term **change** with regards to the Lieutenant. There is some discussion of the way the Lieutenant is presented by Greene.

⚠ Think carefully! What could you do to answer this question more fully? Consider these points:

- Remember to focus on the key term of the question – mention it in your answer.
- Refer explicitly to the writer's technique by bringing Greene into your response – e.g. 'Greene describes the Priest as . . .'
- Are there other characters who might have changed having met the Priest? Consider the mestizo, Luis and Mr Tench.
- What about characters whose behaviour doesn't change? Does the Priest affect the Lehrs?

ACTIVITY 36

Answering a free-standing essay question

1. Note down some bullet points of your own for the question and organise them into a logical structure.
2. Now, go ahead and answer the question.

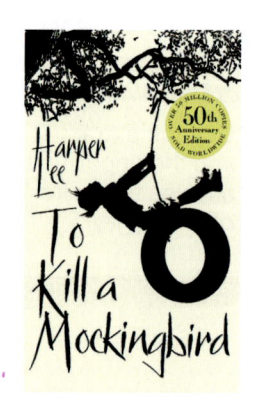

To Kill a Mockingbird by Harper Lee

You will find both the extract and Mark Schemes for these questions on the CCEA website (www.ccea.org.uk).

> **H** With reference to the ways Lee **presents** the children and their father in the extract and elsewhere in the novel, show how far you agree that the children's ideas about Atticus **change**.

Here is part of a Band 2 response:

Aware of character.

Refers to writer's words.

Describes rather than comments.

> The children think that Atticus is 'feeble' because he is old and doesn't play sports with them. Scout asks Miss Maudie questions about her father and doesn't really believe that he is good at anything. Scout is embarrassed by her father 'served to make me even more ashamed of him.'

Let's apply your skills to an extract-based question.

This response is **straightforward**. It shows awareness of the characters but makes no attempt to look at the key terms of the question.

⚠ Think carefully! What could you do to answer this question more successfully? For example:

- How do the children's ideas about Atticus change, for example after the mad-dog incident?
- Discuss the extract in detail – how does Miss Maudie try to make Scout look at her father in a different way?

Let's consider a Band 4 response:

Uses quotation correctly.

Comments on effect of writer's technique.

> In this extract Scout's opinions of her father are obvious and unflattering! She describes him negatively: he is 'feeble', 'Atticus can't do anything', she is 'ashamed of him'. She compares Atticus to other fathers and believes that he couldn't 'possibly arouse the admiration of anyone.'
>
> Lee shows us that she is embarrassed by her father's defence of Tom Robinson and she is not impressed by Miss Maudie's defence of Atticus's abilities. Throughout the extract, we can see Scout's low opinion of her father.

This response is more developed as the student avoids simply describing what happens in the extract and refers explicitly to the use of language. How would you continue this response to show how Scout's attitude changes?

Examiner's tip!
Use the extract. It gives you the opportunity to analyse the writer's use of language.

ACTIVITY 37
Answering an extract-based question

1. Look at both sample responses. Write a plan for the question, taking into account the guidance given.
2. Now, go ahead and answer the question.

Now, let's consider a free-standing essay question.

> **H** With reference to the ways Lee **presents** Calpurnia, show how far you would agree that she is **important** in the Finch household.

Here is part of a Band 2 response:

> Calpurna works as Atticus Finch's housekeeper. She looks after the children and cooks their dinner. This makes her important. Atticus lets her look after the children when he is not there.

Make sure you spell names correctly!

Some awareness of character but 'importance' is just asserted.

This is a **basic** response which shows some awareness of who Calpurnia is.

⚠ Think carefully! What could you do to answer this question more successfully? For example:

- Focus on the key terms of the question – **important**. How is Calpurnia important to the family?
- How is Calpurnia presented by Lee? Think about her role in teaching Scout about manners and discipline and how Atticus defends her to Aunt Alexandra.

Let's consider part of a Band 4 response:

*Sustains focus on **important**.*

> Calpurnia is an important member of the Finch household. She is more than a housekeeper; she cares for the children rather than simply looking after them, we can see this when she talks about 'my children'. She also plays an important role in Scout's development by teaching her about manners. When Walter Cunningham comes to the house for dinner, Calpurnia is described as being 'furious' at Scout's behaviour and punishes her for being rude.

Interprets character.

Some discussion of writer's technique.

This student understands that it is essential to focus on the key terms of the question by considering how Calpurnia is **important** and how this is **presented** by the writer. Consider these questions:

- What are the children's opinions of Calpurnia? Examine their loyalty to her when Aunt Alexandra arrives and how this shows her importance in their eyes.
- What is Calpurnia's role in educating Scout? How can this be linked to the key term **important**?

ACTIVITY 38
Answering a free-standing essay question
1. Look carefully at the bullet points above. Note down your own bullet points.
2. Now, go ahead and answer the essay question.

Examiner's tip!
Bring the writer into it. Discuss **how** Lee describes Calpurnia and her actions.

Bringing it all together

Animal Farm by George Orwell

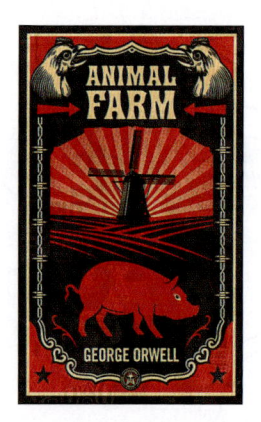

You will find both the extract and Mark Schemes for these questions on the CCEA website (www.ccea.org.uk).

Let's apply your skills to an extract-based question.

> **H** With reference to the ways Orwell **presents** Snowball in the extract and elsewhere in the novel, show how far you would agree that Snowball is an **admirable** figure in the Rebellion until his expulsion from the farm.

Here is part of a Band 2 response:

Comments on character.

*Begins to focus on **admirable**.*

> In this extract we can see that Snowball is the 'most active' in the debates and puts forward resolutions. Snowball organised lots of committees involving the other animals and encouraged the animals to learn to read – 'instituting classes in reading and writing'. Even though his other committees were described as failures, the reading and writing are described as a 'great success'. This is admirable.

Some understanding of writer's use of language.

This student begins to focus on the key term of the question – **admirable** – and refers briefly to the extract, making some comments on character and showing some understanding of the writer's use of language.

! Think carefully! What could you do to answer this question more successfully? For example:

- Can you argue that some of Snowball's actions are **not** admirable? Examine the failure of his committees, and how he does not notice Napoleon's rise to power.
- Discuss the extract in detail – are Snowball's efforts to help the animals understand the Seven Commandments by simplifying them admirable?
- Try to interpret the character of Snowball, based on the extract.
- What contrasts are made by Orwell between Snowball and Napoleon?
- Discuss how Snowball is presented elsewhere – what can you say about his bravery in the Battle of the Cowshed?

Now, let's consider a free-standing essay question.

> **H** With reference to the ways Orwell **presents** the lives of the pigs and the other animals, show how far you would agree that equality for the animals was **impossible**.

ACTIVITY 39
Answering an extract-based question

1. Look carefully at the response and points (right). Write a plan for the question, taking into account the guidance given.
2. Now, go ahead and answer the question.

Examiner's tip!
Use the extract. It gives you the opportunity to analyse the writer's use of language.

Here is part of a Band 2 response:

> The pigs are more important than the other animals because they make the decisions on the farm and can read and write which the other animals can't. They get to keep the apples and milk and the other animals don't get any treats.

Lacks explicit focus on equality being impossible.

Some awareness of events, but not linked to focus of question.

This is a **basic** response showing some awareness of what happens on the farm, but describing the pigs as important rather than looking at the inequality of life on the farm. How could you improve this response?

⚠ Think carefully! What could you do to answer this question more successfully? For example:

- Focus on the key terms of the question – how does Orwell show that equality is **impossible**?
- How does Orwell contrast the other animals' lives to the lives of the pigs as the novel progresses?

A Band 4 answer presents a reasoned response to the question. Look at this sample Band 4 response.

> Life on Animal Farm is one of inequality. The pigs hold the power and control life on the farm so that the other animals depend on the pigs. The fact that the pigs are described as being more intelligent gives them power over the other animals. If the other animals, or even some of them, had been able to master reading and writing competently, then the pigs wouldn't have been able to manipulate them. Therefore, the fact that the pigs can use their intelligence against the rest of the animals means that equality was always going to be impossible.

Some discussion of writer's technique.

Sustained focus on key terms of question.

Interprets events.

Examiner's tip!

Bring the writer into it. Discuss **how** Orwell describes the pigs' lives and contrasts these with the lives of the rest of the animals.

ACTIVITY 40

Answering a free-standing essay question

1. Look carefully at the two bullet points (left). Note down your own bullet points.
2. Now, go ahead and answer the free-standing essay question.

This student presents an argument with selected evidence from the text to support the argument. Consider these questions:

- How does the structure of the novel develop the idea that equality is impossible? Examine how Major's ideals are violated as the novel progresses.
- How does Orwell present the lives of the animals? How does this relate to the key terms of the question?

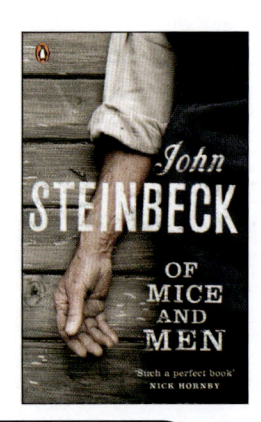

Of Mice and Men by John Steinbeck

You will find both the extract and Mark Schemes for these questions on the CCEA website (www.ccea.org.uk).

Let's apply your skills to an extract-based question.

> **H** With reference to the ways Steinbeck **presents** Candy in the extract and elsewhere in the novel, show how far you agree that Candy is a **pitiable** character.

Here is part of a Band 2 response:

> Candy is pitiable because his only friend is his dog. He spends a lot of time with his dog but it is old and Carlson complains about it. In the extract Carlson complains about the smell of the dog and gets it put down. When this happens Candy is very unhappy and he doesn't speak to anyone.

(Narrative and descriptive response – retelling the story.)

(Some reference to extract, but at a very basic level.)

Think carefully! What could you do to answer this question more successfully? For example:

- Move away from simple description by discussing the key term **pitiable** – **why** is Candy pitiable?
- How has Steinbeck presented Candy as a pitiable character?
- **Comment** on character and events rather than basic narrative.

This Band 4 response is more developed and explicitly considers how Candy has been described in the extract.

> It is clear that Candy's life on the ranch is pitiable. His only companion, an elderly sheepdog, is put down despite Candy's protests. In the extract, Candy is described with degrading words when Carlson suggests shooting his dog, he 'squirmed uncomfortably' and looks 'helplessly' at Slim, hoping that he will stand up for him. This is pitiable because Candy doesn't appear to have enough authority to be able to stand up for himself against Carlson and has to give in 'hopelessly'.

(Focuses on key term.)
(Comments on effect of use of language.)
(Uses quotation correctly.)
(Point developed.)

Remember to discuss technique – what **effect** is the writer is trying to create by choosing words like 'squirmed' and 'hopelessly'?

Examiner's tip!
Use the extract. It gives you the opportunity to analyse the writer's use of language.

ACTIVITY 41
Answering an extract-based question

1. Look carefully at the responses and points above. Write a plan for the question, taking into account the guidance given.
2. Now, go ahead and answer the question.

Now, let's consider a free-standing essay question.

> **H** With reference to the ways Steinbeck **presents** the ranch workers, show how far you agree that their lives are **lonely**.

A Band 2 answer is **basic** and lacks depth, for example:

> George and Lennie are the only ones on the ranch who aren't lonely because they have each other. Candy is lonely because he has to work on his own all day and he only has a dog as a friend. Curley's wife is a lonely character too because she wanders about the ranch looking for someone to talk to and the men treat her badly and call her names.

- Basic comment.
- Lists ideas – these points need to be developed.
- Aware of characters and events.

Think carefully! What could you do to answer this question more fully? For example:

- Explain ideas in more depth by focusing on the key term **presents** – how does Steinbeck describe the ranch workers' lives?
- Can you develop an argument? Are all the ranch workers lonely?

Here is part of a Band 4 response:

> The theme of loneliness is clear in the novel. When George and Lennie arrive at the ranch, they are met with surprise and suspicion as the men on the ranch wonder what motive they have for travelling together. The boss wants to know why George is with Lennie, he suspects George is stealing his pay. 'You takin' his pay away from him?' His suspicion shows that people are used to the lonely life of an itinerant worker and George and Lennie's friendship is unusual.
>
> George himself speaks repeatedly about the loneliness of being a ranch worker – 'guys like us . . . are the loneliest guys in the world.'

- Interprets events.
- Sustains focus on **loneliness**.
- Some discussion of writer's technique.
- Uses quotation correctly.

This student could go on to consider:

- the words 'show how far' – is there an argument that George and Lennie are **not** lonely? How could this be developed?
- what other characters should be examined – Candy, Slim and Crooks?

ACTIVITY 42
Answering a free-standing essay question

1 Look at the responses and points above. Write a plan for the question, taking into account the guidance given.
2 Now, go ahead and answer the question.

Examiner's tip!
Bring the writer into it. Discuss **how** Lee shows that the ranch workers are lonely.

Unit 2

The Study of Drama and Poetry
Section A: Drama

Introduction

Studying drama texts

The theatre

Although your chosen play is a text for study, you must remember that it was intended for the theatre, and you should if possible see a theatre production of your play. This will not only improve your knowledge of the plot and characters, but also deepen your understanding of the dramatic methods and theatrical techniques which are used. Remember that the words are only one part of the dramatist's methods. We shall look at this in more detail in the section in this unit on 'Use of language' (pages 66–69).

Conflict

For drama to hold the attention of the audience, there must be conflict of some kind. A play in which the characters agreed with each other throughout would not be very entertaining! The conflict can be physical, as when Mercutio fights Tybalt in *Romeo and Juliet*, or it can be verbal, as when Linda tries to persuade Mickey to give up his pills in *Blood Brothers*. It can even be between two sides of a single character, as when Macbeth battles with himself about whether or not to kill Duncan.

> **ACTIVITY 1**
>
> **Conflict in your chosen play**
>
> 1 Identify the main conflicts in your chosen play and put them in order of importance.
> 2 Select a few key quotations which sum up each conflict and/or the differing attitudes of the characters involved.
> 3 Write a paragraph on each of these conflicts.

You will need to consider two key questions:

- **Why did the dramatist write this play?** You need to be aware of the themes or issues that they wanted to explore.
- **What techniques did the dramatist use in writing this play?** You have to be able to identify and comment on the various skills and techniques used by the dramatist to make the drama interesting and effective, such as character development or theatrical techniques.

In other words, when studying a play for examination you are expected to show close engagement with all aspects of that text, and to show an awareness and understanding of the dramatist's purpose and skills.

Key features of drama texts

Before arriving in the examination hall, you need to have a thorough, detailed knowledge and understanding of the text. This will come from classroom experiences, personal study, essay practice and revision, and possibly internet research. If you are going to discuss and evaluate a play thoroughly, the most important aspects are:

- **Plot** – the sequence of events that forms the storyline
- **Themes** – the important issues that the playwright wants to explore
- **Characters** – and the relationships between them, and how they develop
- **Language and style** – use of dialogue, imagery, various types of language
- **Dramatic techniques** – such as staging.

These key features will be considered in more detail in the following chapters, and there will be comments on the play you are studying.

What kind of questions will be asked?

In the Drama unit (Unit 2: Section A), you will be assessed on your:

- knowledge and understanding of the play you have studied
- understanding of the techniques the dramatist has used.

Foundation or Higher tier? – An important choice

F Foundation tier questions are slightly more straightforward than Higher tier questions. They also provide more help as they include bullet points which direct you to relevant and important areas of the play. The downside is that at Foundation tier the highest grade you can achieve is a Grade C.

H Higher tier questions are more complex. They may encourage you to look at both sides of an argument, or the question may have an additional part. Higher tier questions have no bullet points, so there is little guidance about relevant areas of the play to discuss. (It is not true to say that there is *no* guidance, as we shall see when we unpack a Higher tier question.) At Higher tier you can be rewarded with a grade up to Grade A*.

The examiner does not want to surprise you. When you know the question types in advance, you are more likely to produce your best work.

You can compare sample Foundation tier and Higher tier questions in the 'Bringing it all together' section (pages 70–73).

Which question?

The Drama unit (Unit 2: Section A) of the examination is 'open book'. This means you may bring an **unannotated** copy of the **prescribed** edition of the play you have studied into the examination. You can choose to answer a **character-focused** question or a **theme-focused** question, but perhaps the more important choice is between the **extract-based question** and the **free-standing essay**. You should think of the advantages of each question type (and of course practise both types).

Character-focused or theme-focused question?

For each of the prescribed drama texts in this examination, there is a choice of questions.

The **(a)** question will ask for a **character-focused** essay. This should **not** be a general character 'sketch' or description. You must present your ideas about a character (or characters) in response to the specific question set.

The **(b)** question will ask for a **theme-focused** essay. You will have to present your ideas about a particular theme or issue that is a strong feature of the text. You will already know from a detailed study of your play what its main themes are.

'Character-focused versus theme-focused'

Here are two questions on *Macbeth*. At Foundation tier there will be bullet points to help you.

> **(H) (a)** With reference to the ways Shakespeare **presents** Macbeth, show how far you agree that Macbeth is **evil**.

This question asks you to look at Macbeth but not just to write a general description of his character. You would need to focus your answer on his evil qualities and perhaps also give a counter argument.

> **(H) (b)** Look again at *Macbeth* Act 1 Scene 3.
>
> With reference to the ways Shakespeare **presents** the witches in this scene, and elsewhere in the play, show how far you agree that the witches are **frightening** and **powerful**.

This question asks you to look at the theme of the supernatural in the play. But note that the question is specific. You must focus on the frightening and powerful qualities of the witches, not just write about the witches generally.

The extract-based question: challenges and advantages

This question:

- gives you a starting point and gets you going
- chooses some relevant material for you
- demands that you deal with the extract in detail. (To do well you will need to consider carefully the question of **presentation** – the dramatic techniques – in the extract.)

In your answer you will need to **balance** use of the extract and 'elsewhere in the play'.

(F) At Foundation tier, bullet points will help you, guiding you into relevant and useful areas of the play and suggesting an effective order for you to deal with the material.

(H) There are no bullet points at Higher tier so you will need to **plan your answer**, allowing time to deal with both extract and 'elsewhere in the play'. You will also have to decide whether or not to start with the extract (most students do). To some extent, strong work in one area may compensate for less thorough work in another, but remember, both extract and 'elsewhere in the play' need to be discussed in response to the specific question.

Remember: If you choose the extract-based question, it is up to you to use the extract properly.

The free-standing essay: challenges and advantages
This question:

- may give you a quicker start
- gives you freedom to choose your own material
- lets you deal with the question of presentation in a more general way.

Considering the writer's skill and technique

What does 'presents' mean?
Whether you choose the extract-based question or the free-standing essay, you must attend to the key term **presents**. With no extract you will do this in a more general way, discussing such features as characterisation, contrast and repetition. (Though, of course, any specific references or quotations you can provide will be valuable.) With an extract-based question, you can deal with the playwright's presentation in the extract in a detailed way, and then refer to the presentation 'elsewhere in the play' in a more general fashion.

The eight set texts in the Drama unit (Unit 2: Section A)
In the Drama unit of the English Literature examination, the eight set texts are:

- *Dancing at Lughnasa* by Brian Friel (see pages 74–75)
- *All My Sons* by Arthur Miller (see pages 76–77)
- *Juno and the Paycock* by Sean O'Casey (see pages 78–79)
- *An Inspector Calls* by J.B. Priestley (see pages 80–81)
- *Blood Brothers* by Willy Russell (see pages 82–83)
- *Macbeth* by William Shakespeare (see pages 84–85)
- *Romeo and Juliet* by William Shakespeare (see pages 86–87)
- *The Merchant of Venice* by William Shakespeare (see pages 88–89)

You are required to study **one** of the texts.

Introduction

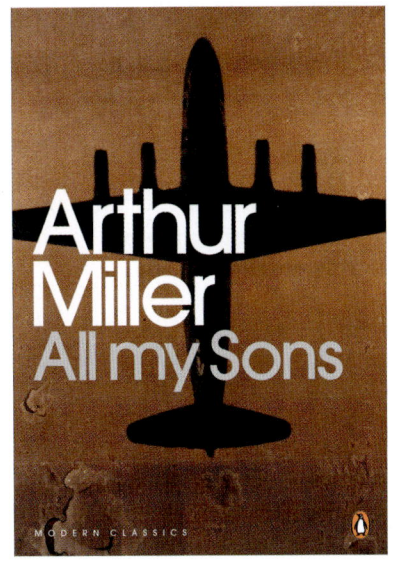

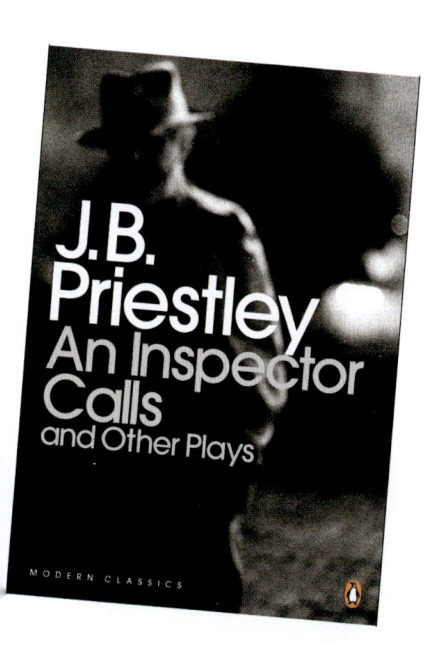

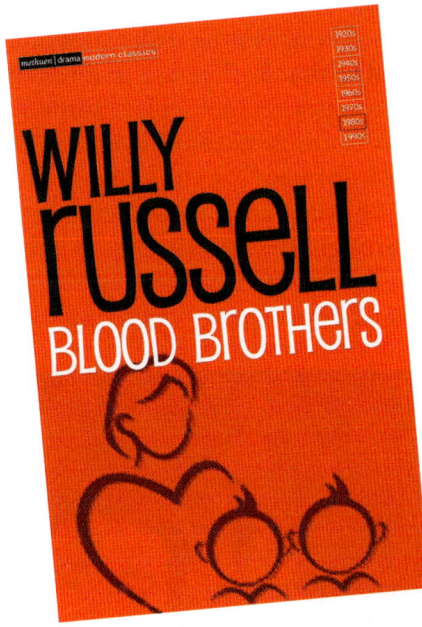

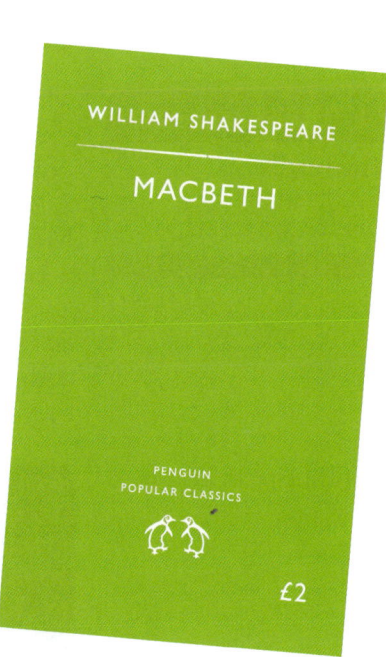

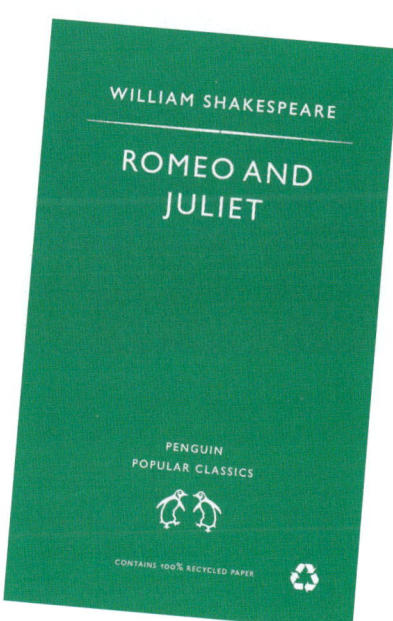

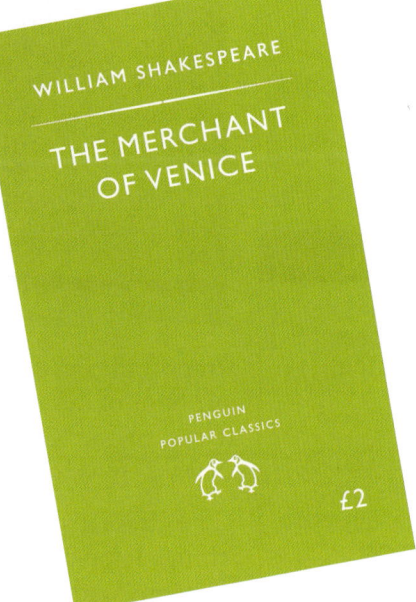

49

1 Plot and structure

Key Words

Plot
The linked sequence of events that forms the storyline

Structure
How a playwright develops and divides the story into different segments

The first interest of anyone in the audience watching a play is probably the plot – in other words, what **happens**.

A 'linked sequence of events' means that the events are connected with each other, from the beginning to the end. We call this linkage **structure**, or **plot structure**. Because the events are linked, they give us a satisfying and complete story.

By the end of this section, you will find that we are discussing not only the 'linked series of events' of the play, but also **why** dramatists shape stories in the particular ways they do.

Sequence

Key Words

Flashback
Events in the past **presented** on stage

Many plays follow a simple **chronological sequence**, where the events of the story are presented in the order in which they happen. Some plays – but not all – use **flashback**. There is interesting use of flashback in *Dancing at Lughnasa*, which is a memory play framed by the speeches of the narrator, Michael, as he reminisces about events in his childhood. Willy Russell uses a kind of 'flash forward' at the start of *Blood Brothers*, where the ending is 'given away'. Shakespeare does something similar at the beginning of *Romeo and Juliet*, through the words of the Chorus. This technique gives the audience an idea of what happens in the play and their attention is held as they watch to see how these events unfold.

Dancing at Lughnasa

Key Words

Reportage
Events in the past **described** by the characters

Climax
The moment, usually at the end of the play, when dramatists make their point most forcefully

Important events in the past may also be **described**, for example Sheila's account of her bad behaviour towards Eva in Milward's shop in *An Inspector Calls*, or Joe Keller's description of the emergency in the factory in *All My Sons*. This is sometimes called **reportage**.

The dramatist will pay close attention to sequence – the order in which things happen. Events can be sequenced so as to lead up to a **climax**. This happens with the appalling crimes that Macbeth commits which lead to his death at the end of the play.

Beginnings and endings

These are important to the structure of the plot. Obviously, the **beginning** of the play is likely to be when the dramatist tries to engage the audience's attention most urgently. *All My Sons* begins near the end of a sequence of events that started long before with Joe Keller's dishonesty. The play then explores the past. *An Inspector Calls* has a similar structure: the events which are so damaging to the characters happened some time before the opening of the play. Now it is time to pay. What do you think are the advantages of a structure such as this?

> **ACTIVITY 2**
> **Beginnings**
>
> In groups, discuss the beginning of your chosen play:
> 1 Explore how the dramatist is trying to engage and interest the audience.
> 2 How successful do you find this opening? Give reasons for your opinions.

> **ACTIVITY 3**
> **Endings**
>
> In groups, discuss the ending of your chosen play:
> 1 Is the ending clearly linked to the previous events of the play?
> 2 Does it contain a climax?
> 3 Does it involve the major character or characters of the play, or minor ones, or even new ones? Comment on this.

Acts and scenes

A play, unless it is very short, is usually divided into a number of 'acts', each of which deals with a phase of the action. These acts may or may not be subdivided into shorter scenes which focus on different aspects of the plot. For example, in Act 3 of *The Merchant of Venice*, two key strands of the plot are developed as the action moves between Venice, where Antonio's life is in danger, and Belmont, with Bassanio and Portia. These scenes are linked by the device of Antonio's letter, so that the action does not become too disjointed.

Repetition and contrast

The use of repetition and contrast can be important in the structure of a play. For example, Macbeth has two encounters with the witches, but it is not simple repetition – there is a contrast in these scenes: the first time, they seek him out, but the second time he goes looking for them. His character has deteriorated so that now he needs the help of the dark forces. You could also consider Joxer Daly's repeated returns to Boyle's household in *Juno and the Paycock*.

Macbeth and the witches

Reviewing the plot structure of your chosen play

The following activities focus on plot structure. Complete the tasks for the play you have studied.

ACTIVITY 4

Dancing at Lughnasa – plot structure

1. The older Michael makes five speeches in the play. Write a few sentences about each of these speeches, summarising what Michael says.
2. Consider **where** these speeches are made in the play. Why do you think Friel placed Michael's speeches at these points?
3. The older Michael plays no part in the action of the drama. Why is he an important character?

ACTIVITY 5

All My Sons – plot structure

1. In this play, past events are reported by different characters. Find the speeches in Act 1 and Act 2 describing the emergency in Keller's factory three years before the action of the play. (There are two by Joe Keller and one by George Deever.)
2. Make notes on each version of events and explain clearly why each man says what he does.

ACTIVITY 6

Juno and the Paycock – plot structure

1. Look at the way the play is divided into acts. Summarise briefly what happens in each act.
2. Does each act take the plot forward or show a different aspect of events? Put your opinions about this into a short paragraph.
3. Now look at the ending of the play, from where Boyle and Joxer, 'both of them very drunk', enter. This short scene seems to add nothing to the play. Suggest some reasons why O'Casey chose to end his play in this way.

ACTIVITY 7

An Inspector Calls – plot structure

1. The Inspector's investigation is complete and he leaves less than halfway into Act 3. Is his departure the climax of the play? Give your reasons.
2. How does Priestley keep up the audience's interest from this point until the final curtain?

ACTIVITY 8

Blood Brothers – plot structure

1. Look at the ending of Act 1 from the stage direction *Mrs Johnstone appears, clutching a letter*. From what Mrs Johnstone says and does, describe her state of mind.
2. Why do you think Russell placed this scene just before the interval between Acts 1 and 2?

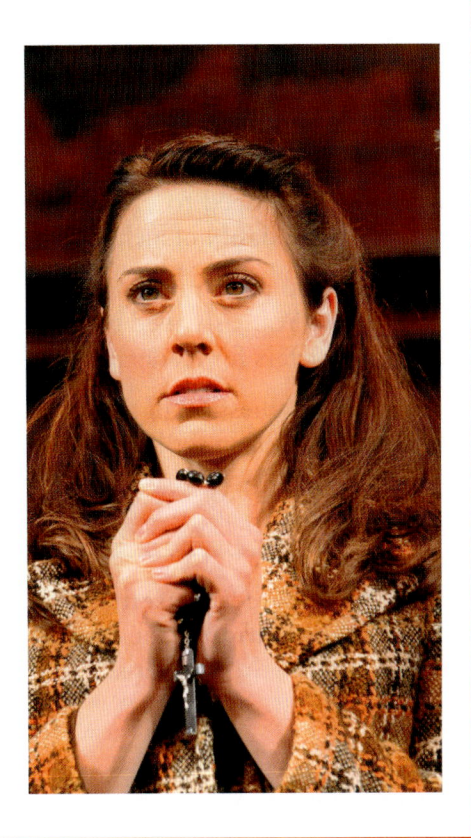

ACTIVITY 9

Macbeth – plot structure

1. Read the opening scene of the play. Write down what we learn about the witches in this scene.
2. Why did Shakespeare choose to begin the play with the witches, rather than introduce us immediately to Macbeth?

ACTIVITY 10

Romeo and Juliet – plot structure

'In Act 1 Scene 1 of the play we first meet unimportant minor characters, and then gradually Shakespeare introduces more important characters.'

1. Show how far you agree with this statement.
2. What are Shakespeare's intentions in beginning the play in this way?

ACTIVITY 11

The Merchant of Venice – plot structure

1. Think about the climax or climaxes of this play. Look at the trial scene, Act 4 Scene 1. Where, in your opinion, is the climax of this scene? Give your reasons.
2. What about Act 5 Scene 1? Is there a climax in this the final scene of the play? If so, where? Is the scene a disappointing anticlimax after the tension of the trial?

Review

Let's review some of the key words and ideas used in this chapter:

- plot
- structure
- chronological sequence
- flashback
- reportage
- climax
- repetition
- contrast.

Make sure you understand each term clearly. Make a list of definitions which you can use for revision.

2 Characterisation

What is 'character'?

Obviously the characters are the personages of the play. But when you are asked to write about characters, you must give more than a simple description. You need to examine **characterisation** – how the dramatist reveals the personality of a character and presents it on stage.

This means you must remember that characters are deliberately created by the dramatist. You also need to be aware of the ways playwrights create and develop characters for readers and the audience.

There will be a question in the examination which focuses on character. At **H** tier, this question will usually start with the words:

> With reference to the ways the dramatist **presents** [the named character] . . .

The key word here is **presents**. This is in the question to encourage you to focus on the **techniques** the dramatist uses to create character. Remember: the discussion of the dramatist's technique is one of the secrets of success in this examination.

Getting to know the characters

We usually enjoy a play if the characters are believable and interesting. We sometimes say they are 'flesh and blood' or 'three-dimensional' characters to show our interest and approval. Some of the characters in the plays you may have studied are unforgettable – Joxer Daly, for example, or Shylock, or Maggie Mundy or Inspector Goole. But remember, they are not real people, they are creations of the dramatist!

You need to be able to describe such characters – their appearance, what they do, what happens to them, and their motivation. All of this is a good basis of knowledge, but it is only a start. To move up the grades you need to go further than description, to understand how the dramatist has **created and presented** the characters on stage.

Let's start with **description**. This is a starting exercise you should do for all the main characters in your chosen play.

Key Word

Characterisation
The ways a dramatist conveys information to help the reader or audience form a complete impression of a character

Examiner's tip!

Focus on the dramatist's technique in your answer by discussing the use of words and phrases, imagery, interactions with other characters, and stage directions.

Shylock

Inspector Goole

ACTIVITY 12

Describing a character

Create a concept map for the character, noting:

- name of character
- physical details
- their background
- social position or work
- what you learn from what they say and do
- what you learn from what other characters say or how other characters react
- how the character changes or develops in the course of the play
- what the narrator or chorus says about them (if relevant)
- your reactions to them, and why.

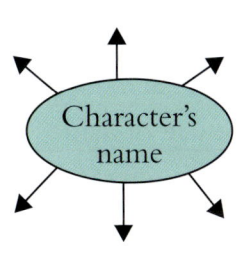

Presentation

No matter how thorough your work on Activity 12, an answer to the character question in your examination that uses these points alone is not likely to score high in the Mark Bands. This is because this question will be focused not just on a description of a character, but also on how the character is **presented**. So you must take care to use the information collected in Activity 12 to focus on presentation. In that way you can be sure to move up the grades.

You need to look at how the dramatist uses various techniques to present the characters you described in Activity 12 – how the dramatist uses dialogue, for example, or staging.

ACTIVITY 13

Dramatist's techniques

Copy and complete the following table for one of the characters you described in Activity 12. Be careful – not all of the headings or all of the bullet points will apply to your chosen play/character.

First impressions • How the character is introduced to the audience on their first appearance	
The use of stage directions • Background information • Physical appearance or personal facts • Instructions on how actors should deliver particular lines • Instructions on movement, lighting or sound effects	

The use of dialogue • What the character says to others • How others reply • Voice tones • Speech mode, e.g. formal or informal, dialect	
The use of asides or soliloquies	
What a narrator or chorus says about the character	
The use of language • How this reflects the character's mood and that of others • How personality is revealed through the character's choice of language, e.g. the imagery they use • Use of humour • Use of colloquial or formal speech, prose, verse or song	
The use of setting • The importance of location to the character • How the historical setting helps us understand the character • How the social setting helps us understand the character	
The use of actions • What the character does • How others react • The pace of the action	

If you compare the information you collect in Activities 12 and 13 you will notice a lot of overlap, but you should also notice an important difference. You are starting to focus on the dramatist and the techniques used in presenting the character.

Let's look at a sample question based on *Dancing at Lughnasa*.

> **H** With reference to the ways Friel **presents** Gerry Evans, show how far you agree that Gerry Evans is **unreliable**.

If you were writing a character sketch, you would mention all the important qualities that make up Gerry's personality – his charm for example, or his entertaining manner. But the second key term in the question is **unreliable**, and that is what you must focus on here.

Here is part of a Band 3 response to the question:

> We know from the stage directions that Gerry smiles all the time, and has an English accent, which might have impressed Chris. He is very polite when he is speaking to Chris but it comes out that he has not seen her for over a year. For all that time she has been looking after his child with no support from him. In this way he is certainly unreliable.
>
> He says, 'Tell her I was asking for her – Agnes . . .' and I think he would like to have a relationship with Agnes. He asks Agnes to dance with him near the end of the play and kisses her. I think Chris, who is the mother of his child, should come first, and so here again he is unreliable.

Makes some comment on dramatist's technique but could have developed these remarks.

Begins to develop an argument.

*Focus (on **unreliability**) is better than development of argument.*

Here is part of a Band 4 response:

> Gerry arrives unexpectedly and the sisters get very excited when he appears. He tells Chris that he had planned to come to Ballybeg many times, but that he had got a lift from a man in a bar the previous night. Friel uses the detail that he was in a bar to suggest his unreliable nature. He spends money on drink, but Chris gets nothing to look after Michael.
>
> Friel gives us a lot of information about how Gerry looks and talks. He can tell silly stories in a very amusing way, like the story about the one-horned cow that winked at him. Chris can't really get angry at him, but these stories, and his fashionable cane, straw hat and the English accent that probably impressed Chris a lot when she first met him can not make us forget that he got Chris pregnant and then ran away. Michael's bicycle that never arrives is another of Friel's ways of showing us that Gerry just can't be relied on.
>
> However, we need to remember that Gerry does ask Chris to marry him. He seems to mean it, 'I'm mad about you. You know I am.' Chris turns him down. She knows he is not reliable. In the same conversation Friel makes Gerry say, 'Wales isn't my home any more' but later we find out that he had a second family back in Wales. I think this shows how unreliable he is.

*Using dramatist's name helps to focus on **presentation**.*

Pays attention to effects of dramatic technique.

Develops answer by suggesting counter argument.

Sustained focus. Uses key term in every paragraph.

Review

Let's review some of the key words and ideas used in this section:

- **characterisation**
- **key terms in question**
- **dialogue**
- **stage directions**.

Make sure you understand each term clearly. Make a list of definitions which you can use for revision.

3 Stage directions and dramatic techniques

> **ACT I**
>
> The dining-room of the Birlings' house in Brumley, an industrial city in the North Midlands. An evening in Spring, 1912
>
> It is the dining-room of a fairly large suburban house, belonging to a prosperous manufacturer; a solidly built square room, with good solid furniture of the period. There is only one door, which is up stage in the L. wall. Up stage C., set in an alcove, is a heavy sideboard with a silver tantalus, silver candlesticks, a silver champagne cooler and the various oddments of a dinner. The fireplace is in the R. wall. Below the door is a desk with a chair in front of it. On the wall below the fireplace is a telephone. Slightly up stage of C. is a solid but not too large dining-table, preferably oval, with a solid set of dining-room chairs round it. The table is laid with a white cloth and the closing stages of a dinner. Down stage of the fireplace is a leather armchair. A few imposing but tasteless pictures and large engravings decorate the walls, and there are light brackets above and below the fireplace and below the door. The former are lit, but the latter is not. The general effect is substantial and comfortable and old-fashioned, but not cosy and home-like
> (See the Ground Plan at the end of the play)
>
> When the CURTAIN rises, Edna, a neatly dressed parlourmaid is clearing the table of dessert plates and finger bowls, taking them to the sideboard. Arthur Birling is seated R. of the table, and Mrs Birling are L. Sheila Birling and Gerald Croft are seated above the table, R. and L. respectively. Eric Birling sits below the table. All five are in evening dress, the men in tails and white ties. Arthur Birling is a heavy-looking, rather portentous man in his middle fifties, with fairly easy manners but rather provincial in his speech. His wife is about fifty, a rather cold woman and her husband's social superior. Sheila is a pretty girl in her early twenties, very pleased with life and rather excited. Gerald Croft is an attractive chap about thirty, rather too manly to be a dandy but very much the easy well-bred young man-about-town. Eric is in his middle twenties, not quite at ease, half-shy, half-assertive. At the moment they have all had a good dinner, are celebrating a special occasion, and are pleased with themselves
>
> **Birling** Giving us the port, Edna?
>
> *Edna comes to Birling's L. with the decanter*
>
> That's right. (*He fills his glass and pushes it towards Sheila*) You ought to like this port Gerald. As a matter of fact, Finchley told me it's exactly the same port your father gets from him.
>
> *Sheila fills her glass and passes the port to Gerald*

When you read a play in class, never forget that it was written for performance. In the examination, you will be asked to consider the use of dramatic techniques and if you want to move up the grades, you must give some attention to them.

Dramatic techniques is a very wide topic. Most of the tasks in this section are based on stage directions.

Stage directions

Stage directions vary from play to play. For example the location at the start of *Macbeth* is described in only three words – *A desert heath* – whereas Priestley gives us over a page of stage directions at the start of *An Inspector Calls*.

We take in stage directions as we read a play, but remember that they are directed not just at us, but at those who work at presenting the play – the director, designers, technicians and actors. Stage directions show how the dramatist's script can be 'brought to life'.

In older plays, such as Shakespeare's, the stage directions are often embedded in the characters' speeches rather than printed separately, so a character, rather than a stage direction, tells us (as Friar Lawrence does in *Romeo and Juliet*) that the sun has just come up, or that someone is carrying a sword.

ACTIVITY 14
Stage directions

In the play that you are studying find examples of stage directions, either printed or embedded, for as many of the following as you can:

- actor's movement
- how an actor should deliver a speech
- props
- lighting
- sound
- setting.

(Not all will appear in your chosen play.)

ACTIVITY 15
Dancing at Lughnasa – group discussion

Watch out for:

- the care with which Friel describes set and costume
- lighting instructions, e.g. suggesting *a warm summer afternoon*
- frequent stage directions indicating actors' movements
- stage directions indicating how actors should deliver particular lines or speeches
- use of the narrator (Michael), and of the boy Michael
- use of props – especially the radio.

In groups discuss:

1. How does Friel use the long stage direction for the dance in Act 1 (pages 21–22) to show us differences between the sisters?
2. Look at the stage directions at the beginning and end of the play. What do you think are Friel's intentions here?
3. Write up your conclusions into a paragraph for each topic.

ACTIVITY 16

All My Sons – group discussion

Watch out for:

- the care with which Miller describes the set at the start of the play
- descriptions of characters and how they are dressed
- use of props – the broken tree, the letter
- frequent stage directions indicating actors' movements, and how they should deliver particular lines or speeches
- offstage sound effects – Ann's voice on the phone, the pistol shot
- lighting effects – Ann's window.

In groups discuss the dramatic uses which Miller makes of the broken tree.

ACTIVITY 17

Juno and the Paycock – group discussion on stage directions, then write up your own notes

Watch out for:

- O'Casey's description of the set at the beginning of each act
- the sometimes lengthy descriptions of characters, how they are dressed, the way they walk
- frequent stage directions indicating actors' movements, and how they should deliver particular lines or speeches
- use of songs and poems – to suggest Boyle's foolish sentimentality, or Joxer's scanty repertoire
- use of props – bottle of stout, gramophone
- offstage sound effects – Tancred's funeral.

Write a paragraph on the use of the props mentioned above. Why does O'Casey include them?

ACTIVITY 18

An Inspector Calls – group discussion on stage directions, then write up your own notes

Watch out for:

- the careful description of the set at the beginning of Act 1 – props and costume indicate social and historical setting
- stage directions used to describe characters
- frequent stage directions indicating actors' movements, and how they should deliver particular lines or speeches
- use of lighting – when the Inspector arrives
- use of sound effects – doorbell, slamming door
- use of props – photograph, telephone, engagement ring, decanter.

Write short paragraphs on Priestley's use of the props listed above.

Stage directions/dramatic techniques

59

ACTIVITY 19

Blood Brothers **– group discussion on stage directions, then write up your own notes**

Watch out for:

- Willy Russell's 'Production Note' on the set
- uses of the Narrator – to ask questions, comment on action, take part in action, indicate future events
- sung monologues – when Mrs Johnstone introduces herself (she has her own melody, which is repeated later), the Narrator's 'Shoes upon the table'
- swapping of roles, so that an actor may play more than one character
- use of props – cushion, Bible, toy and real guns
- use of imagined props – the bus in Act 2
- use of sound effects, particularly involving music, e.g. bass note repeated as heartbeat as the pact is agreed. Can you think of others? What are their effects?
- use of mime.

In groups discuss and make notes on the various dramatic techniques used in the climax of the play, when the twins die.

Shakespeare

Shakespeare's plays contain only a few stage directions, some of which were added by later editors. There are, however, plenty of 'embedded' stage directions where it is quite clear what Shakespeare intended an actor to do from what is said on stage.

Macbeth

In *Macbeth* special stage effects may be used in the presentation of the supernatural, and of the opposed armies in the battle scenes. Notice the embedded stage direction about the witches' physical appearance when Banquo sees them for the first time. There are also frequent exits and entrances in the battle scenes of Act 5 as Shakespeare increases the pace of the play towards its climax.

Obvious props are the 'ingredients' of the witches' cauldron, Lady Macbeth's letter and the daggers which Macbeth uses to kill Duncan.

Obvious sound effects are the battle noises at the end of the play, or the screaming owl and the knocking at the gate which do so much to create

ACTIVITY 20

Macbeth **– the supernatural**

1. Look carefully at Macbeth's encounters with the supernatural.
2. Write a few paragraphs on the dramatic techniques Shakespeare uses in these scenes. Make sure what you say is based on the text.

atmosphere in the murder scene. The chanting of the witches seems intended to increase their impact by setting them apart.

Many speeches are marked 'aside', which is understandable in a play where there is so much plotting and mistrust.

Several characters are given soliloquies, speeches where no other character is present. These are rather like voiceovers in a film, letting us know what a character is really thinking.

Romeo and Juliet

The stage directions in *Romeo and Juliet* tell us of a large number of servants, 'maskers', torch-bearers and musicians. These 'extras' convey the business and bustle of great families and of the streets of the city. Many of the stage directions are embedded, so that, for example, we learn of the darkness of the churchyard from what Paris and his page say.

As props, knives and swords are often mentioned, suggesting that violence was never far away in Verona.

> **ACTIVITY 21**
>
> **Romeo and Juliet – danger and excitement**
>
> 1. Look at the opening of the play, up to the entrance of Prince Escalus.
> 2. Write a paragraph about how Shakespeare presents the danger and excitability of life on the street.

The Merchant of Venice

Watch out for:

- use of costume – Jessica in disguise and Lorenzo masked, Portia disguised as a lawyer. Note the possible embedded stage direction in Shylock's reference to Antonio spitting on his 'Jewish gaberdine'.
- use of sound effects – a 'flourish of cornets' shows the importance of the arrivals of Morocco and Arragon. This does not happen with Bassanio. Music accompanies Bassanio's pondering on the caskets, and is also playing when Portia returns to Belmont.
- use of props – the caskets, letters used at important moments in the plot.
- use of asides – by the anxious Portia as Bassanio chooses his casket.
- use of lighting – there is a famous embedded stage direction about the moonlight in the garden at the beginning of Act 5.

> ### Review
>
> Let's review some of the key words and ideas used in this section:
>
> - props
> - asides
> - soliloquies
> - embedded stage directions.
>
> Make sure you understand each term clearly. Make a list of definitions which you can use for revision.

> **Key Words**
>
> **Soliloquy**
> The character is usually alone on stage. Some soliloquies, as in *Macbeth*, can be quite long. We learn the truth about what the speaker is thinking.
>
> **Aside**
> The speaker is not alone on stage but breaks off a conversation to make a remark to the audience which other characters do not hear.

> **ACTIVITY 22**
>
> **The Merchant of Venice – discussion and presentation**
>
> 'There is more to *The Merchant of Venice* than just the words. Shakespeare provides us with all-round entertainment for the eyes, ears and mind.'
>
> In groups, discuss this statement and present your conclusions to the class.

> **Key Word**
>
> **Themes**
> The main ideas explored in a play

4 Themes

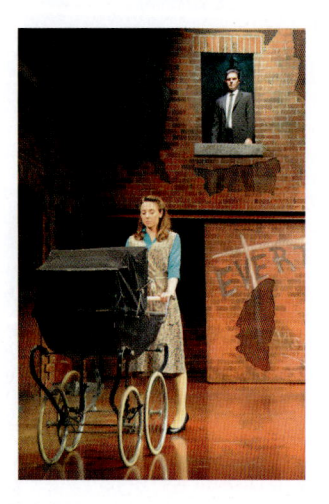

The dramatist's first job is to please and interest the audience, but as we watch or read a play, we gradually realise that there are ideas behind the story which the dramatist is exploring; these are the **themes**. A play may have more than one theme.

It is important to be clear about the differences between the plot and the themes of a play. For example, *Blood Brothers* tells the story of how a poor mother gave away one of her twins to be brought up in a rich family. This is the **plot**, the linked series of events. However, the dramatist, Russell, is interested in certain issues which the plot conveys. We could say that he is interested in fate, superstition and social class. These more general issues are **themes**.

Similarly, *Macbeth* tells the story of how a soldier turned against his king, murdered him and took the crown. This is the **plot**. However, Shakespeare is interested in exploring certain issues through the plot – for example, temptation and ambition. These more general issues are the **themes**.

Blood Brothers

Writer's technique

In the examination there will be a question based on a theme in the play you have studied. The theme is often printed in bold type to help you to focus on it. Here is an example of a **theme-focused** question on *Macbeth*:

> H With reference to the ways Shakespeare **presents** the thoughts and actions of Macbeth and his wife, show how far you would agree that they are driven by **ambition**.

The dramatist will explore themes in a play through the development of **plot**, **character**, **use of language** and **staging**.

In *Macbeth*, Shakespeare explores the theme of ambition through:

- **Plot** – Macbeth's success puts him in a position where he can gain the crown.
- **Character** – Shakespeare explores the theme of ambition through Macbeth's own desires, the prophecies of the witches, and the influence his wife has on him.
- **Use of language** – Macbeth's speeches and their imagery open a window on his ambition for us.
- **Staging** – Macbeth's asides and soliloquies let us know the truth about his ambition.

Here is part of a Band 2 answer to the question opposite:

> Macbeth is very ambitious and wants more than anything else to be king. He is very cruel in battle as we see when he fights Macdonwald and 'unseamed him from the nave to the chaps'. He is cruel also in the way he kills Duncan, who was old and asleep when he was attacked. Macbeth's murders got worse and worse. First it was his best friend Banquo and he ended up killing women and children who could not defend themselves.
>
> The idea of becoming king came from the witches but his wife gave him a heavy time when he came home and soon persuaded him. She told him he was 'infirm of purpose' and made him feel ashamed.

Idea valid, but not developed. No argument.

*Tells story – does not give argument about **ambition** of Macbeth and Lady Macbeth.*

*Quotations presented properly but not made relevant to theme of **ambition**.*

This student uses the key term **ambition**, but then forgets about it and deals with Macbeth's cruelty and how his wife shamed him. The student attempts to focus on the question, but does not succeed. To get into Band 3, this answer needs a more determined focus on the key term and how this ambition is shown in the thoughts and actions of Macbeth and his wife.

Here is part of a Band 4 answer:

Uses key term and takes both characters into consideration.

> This ambitious couple work as a team in the early days. When he is afraid, she is there to push him forward. He says, 'We will proceed no further in this business' when he feels that his ambitions are satisfied by being given the title of Thane of Cawdor, but she comes back at him scornfully, comparing him to the 'poor cat' in the proverb which wanted fish but was afraid to get its paws wet. She uses imagery that will annoy her husband, whose reputation is based on his bravery, and reawakes in him the ambitious plan to grab power.

Suggests counter argument – Macbeth is satisfied with what he has got.

Discusses effect of use of language.

This student repeats 'ambitions' and 'ambitious' to show sustained focus on the key term of the question. This is essential to achieving marks in the higher bands.

Let's look at how a theme is explored in *An Inspector Calls*. In this play, Priestley explores the theme of **responsibility** through:

- **Plot** – A police inspector calls on the Birling family to investigate the death of a young girl.
- **Character** – Priestley explores the theme of responsibility through the differing reactions of the people whom the Inspector questions.
- **Use of language** – Biblical language used by the Inspector in his final speech emphasises the seriousness of failing in our responsibilities.
- **Staging** – The luxurious furnishings of the Birlings' house show the undeserved comfort in which this selfish and irresponsible family are living at the start of the play; the doorbell and telephone act as alarming warnings to the members of the family.

ACTIVITY 23
Identifying themes

Identify two or three themes in the play that you are studying. Make a note of these and then compare your list with the themes suggested below.

Examiner's tip!
Remember to support your ideas with carefully selected words and phrases from the text.

ACTIVITY 24
Investigating themes

Theme	Key incident	Useful words and phrases

1. Copy the table above. Use the themes that you identified in Activity 23 and those listed below for the play that you are studying in the first column.
2. Think of a key incident which develops each theme and **briefly** describe it in the second column.
3. Select useful words and phrases from the text as evidence.

Don't go into too much detail in filling out the second and third columns. It is more important to **select the key incidents** and the **most useful words and phrases**.

Dancing at Lughnasa
- Family life
- Responsibility
- Shame

All My Sons
- Responsibility
- The secrets of the past
- Crime and punishment

Juno and the Paycock
- Strong women and weak men
- Selfishness
- Family life

An Inspector Calls
- Responsibility
- Older and younger generations
- Social class

Blood Brothers
- Fate
- Social class
- Superstition

Macbeth
- Ambition
- Good and bad kings
- The supernatural

Romeo and Juliet
- Love
- Feuding families
- Peacemaking

The Merchant of Venice
- Judging by appearances
- Prejudice
- Friendship

The theme of friendship is clear in *The Merchant of Venice*

> **Examiner's tip!**
>
> Be aware of the wording of the question. For example, a question on *All My Sons* may ask about Joe Keller's 'dishonesty' rather than whether or not he was 'a guilty man'. Get the key term right, and use it.

ACTIVITY 25
Exploring themes

Take some of the themes from your chosen play and explore how the dramatist develops them under the headings:

- Plot
- Character
- Use of language
- Staging

ACTIVITY 26
Writing about themes

Using your notes from Activities 24 and 25, write an extended paragraph on one of the themes of your chosen play. Use brief quotations to illustrate the points you make.

You should repeat this activity for each of the important themes in your chosen play as part of your revision for the examination.

Review

There will be a **theme-focused** question in the examination so it is important to understand the themes in the play you have studied and the **ways** the dramatist has explored each theme. When planning your answer to a theme-focused question, think about the work you have done here and how the dramatist explores themes through **plot**, **character**, **use of language** and **staging**.

5 Use of language

In the examination it is important to consider the dramatist's use of language to address the part of the question that asks you about **presentation**.

Language used in characterisation

Macbeth and Lady Macbeth

Just as in a novel, the characters in a play will not all speak in the same way. Styles of speech vary according to character, and according to the situations in which characters find themselves. For the dramatist, language is a method of characterisation. Think of the 1912 slang used by Eric in *An Inspector Calls*, or the colloquial Donegal speech of Maggie in *Dancing at Lughnasa*, or the North of England urban language used in *Blood Brothers*.

A famous example of language used to reflect the dramatic situation is the gasping, nervous conversation between Macbeth and his wife after the murder of Duncan. The two characters can hardly speak, and Shakespeare shows their panicky state of mind through their fragmentary speech.

The language used may reflect the:

- character of the speaker, their speech habits or state of mind
- situation in which the characters find themselves
- time and/or place where the play is set.

Examination questions

If you choose the **extract-based** question, you will be expected to analyse in detail the ways in which language is used in an extract from your chosen play. A more general discussion of language is acceptable if you choose the **free-standing essay**. But remember, any **relevant** discussion of language will be welcomed by the examiner, as it will address the key term **presentation**.

Watch out for:

- word choices made by the speakers
- imagery
- length/brevity of speeches
- soliloquies and asides
- questions and exclamations
- use of punctuation, interruptions, unfinished sentences.

Use of language in your chosen play

The following activities and the accompanying information encourage you to think about how language is used in your chosen play.

> **ACTIVITY 27**
>
> **Language in your chosen play**
>
> Working in groups or with your teacher, construct a paragraph showing how language is used in your chosen play in one of the three ways listed above: character, situation, time/place.

Dancing at Lughnasa

ACTIVITY 28
Language used in characterisation

Maggie: This character's language is often very colloquial. It often reflects her sense of humour and her liveliness. Frequent scraps of popular songs and jokes reflect her role as an entertainer in the family.

Michael as narrator: The adult Michael speaks Standard English as he is distanced from the 1930s Donegal setting. At the end of the play he speaks movingly of his memories of his Ballybeg aunts.

1. Find examples of the speech of Maggie and the adult Michael that match these descriptions.
2. Write similar descriptions, with examples, of the speech of Kate, Father Jack and Rose.

ACTIVITY 29
Gerry's speech

Make notes on how Gerry speaks in Act 1 when he arrives and meets Chris (page 26).

All My Sons

> It's dollars and cents, nickels and dimes. . ... Half the goddam country is gotta go if I go.

The language in *All My Sons* reflects the America of just after the Second World War with references to contemporary film stars (Don Ameche), cartoons (Andy Gump), and breakfast cereals (Post Toasties). There are a few echoes in Joe Keller's speech of his days on the factory floor ('It changed all the tallies.'). Common Americanisms include: 'I diapered him', 'want ads', 'taking out the garbage', 'depot' (for bus station).

ACTIVITY 30
Period detail

The play is set in the 1930s and the language reflects this.

Find and list examples of the ways Friel uses language to suggest life in the 1930s.

Juno and the Paycock

Notice the differences in the ways the characters speak. In the Boyle household we hear the ordinary speech of the Dublin tenements, but there are differences among the characters:

- Mary never speaks as broadly as Juno or Boyle.
- Joxer's speech is full of catchphrases, proverbs and scraps of song.
- Jerry uses romantic language, but only when speaking to Mary.
- Bentham speaks Standard English, with pretentious references to Eastern philosophy.

ACTIVITY 31
Time and place

Discuss the use of language in the speech by Joe Keller in Act 1 beginning: 'The man was a fool.'

ACTIVITY 33
Repetition

The events leading up to Eva/Daisy's death are gone over several times. Facts and even phrases are repeated.

Find examples and suggest reasons why Priestley does this.

ACTIVITY 32
Poems and songs

Look at some of the poems and songs in the play, for example:

- 'When the robins nest agen' (Boyle, Act 1)
- 'Shawn and I were best friends, sir' (Boyle, Act 2)
- 'To Jesus' heart all burning' (the Crowd, Act 2)
- 'An' we felt the power. . ..' (Mary, Act 3).

In groups, discuss why O'Casey uses each of these songs or poems at this particular point in the play.

ACTIVITY 34
Images

Look at the Inspector's final speech. There are two striking images:

- 'We are members of one body'
- 'If men will not learn that lesson, then they must be taught it in fire and blood and anguish'.

In two paragraphs, write down what Priestley means, and why you think he uses these images.

An Inspector Calls

Priestley mixes long speeches when characters are trying to explain themselves and their treatment of Eva/Daisy, with rapid dialogue when they come under the pressure of the Inspector's interrogation. However, in his confession Eric makes no long speeches. Why do you think Priestley uses these methods?

The Inspector specialises in questions which are really statements – for he knows the answer already: 'You went with her to her lodgings that night?'

Blood Brothers

The language of the play mixes colloquial speech, Standard English, poetry and song.

ACTIVITY 36
Songs

Some of the songs from Act 1 are:

- the 'Marilyn Monroe' song
- 'Only mine until'
- 'Shoes upon the table' (the imagery here is interesting)
- 'I wish I was our Sammy'
- the children's game song: 'But you know if you cross your fingers'
- 'Just pack up the bags'.

In groups, discuss why Russell uses each of these songs at this particular point of the play.

ACTIVITY 35
Standard English

Which characters use Standard English? What reasons might Russell have for making them speak in this way?

Shakespeare

Shakespeare often uses **verse** for the speech of noble or serious characters, and **prose** for common or comic characters.

Soliloquies and **asides** tell us what is going on in a character's mind.

Macbeth

If you are answering the **extract-based** question, you should be prepared to say something about the **imagery** used in this play, for example:

- clothing imagery, which suggests that by becoming king Macbeth has moved up to a level where he does not belong
- repeated images of blood and darkness to convey the growing violence and despair of Macbeth's state of mind.

> **ACTIVITY 37**
>
> **Macbeth's use of language**
>
> > It will have blood, they say; blood will have blood:
> > Stones have been known to move, and trees to speak;
> > Augurs, and understood relations, have
> > By maggot-pies, and choughs, and rooks, brought forth
> > The secret'st man of blood. …
>
> 1 Find out where Macbeth is when he says these words and explain in as much detail as possible why he speaks in this way.
> 2 Why does he repeat the word 'blood' so often?

Romeo and Juliet

Watch out for:

- **Imagery:** Sun, moon and stars imagery is often used: the sun to suggest the rapid passing of time (something the two young lovers are very conscious of); the moon, because it changes all the time, to suggest faithlessness; and the stars to suggest both the beauty of Juliet's eyes and the fate of the 'star-crossed lovers'. There is also contrasting homely imagery used by the Nurse.
- **Exaggeration:** Rather than marry Paris, Juliet says 'chain me with roaring bears'. Look too at the Nurse's exclamations of grief at Juliet's supposed death.
- Sword-fighting terms associated with Mercutio and Tybalt.

The Merchant of Venice

Watch out for:

- **classical imagery**, often used for the love theme – Portia as the Golden Fleece
- **Old Testament imagery** for Shylock's darker story – Jacob, Laban
- the many **memorable images** that sum up a situation – 'Thus hath the candle sing'd the moth', Bassanio's 'lost arrow' image
- use of **rhetoric** (rhetorical questions, exclamations, repetitions) in the court scene and elsewhere.

ACTIVITY 38

A soliloquy and an aside

1 Find one example of a soliloquy and one of an aside in Macbeth.
2 Explain what they tell us and why Shakespeare uses them.

ACTIVITY 39

Romeo's images

List and learn two or three of the images which Romeo uses to describe Juliet.

ACTIVITY 40

Imagery and rhetoric

1 Find further examples in The *Merchant of Venice* for the bullet points (left).
2 Write a paragraph for each.

Review

Let's review some of the key words and ideas used in this section:

- **imagery**
- **rhetoric**
- **colloquial speech**
- **soliloquy**
- **prose and verse**
- **aside**.

Make sure you understand each term clearly. Make a list of definitions which you can use for revision.

Use of language

6 Bringing it all together

Some reminders about the Drama unit (Unit 2: Section A)

What is being assessed?
- Your knowledge and understanding of the play; your ability to develop an argument about it
- Your understanding of the dramatist's technique
- 'Quality of written communication'

Time and planning
You should spend **45 minutes** on the Drama question. You answer **one** question. You can choose to answer either a **theme-focused** or a **character-focused** question on the play you have studied.

It is most important that you **plan** your answer, especially at Higher tier, where there are no guiding bullet points. Beforehand, in class, you should discuss and practise how to manage the 45 minutes for both extract-based and free-standing essay questions. Without planning, your answer is likely to be incoherent. Remember that 'Quality of written communication' is assessed in this examination.

Regulations
This is an 'open-book' section, which means you may bring an **unannotated** copy of the play into the examination. Make sure that you have the **prescribed edition** – otherwise you may find it difficult to find the extract.

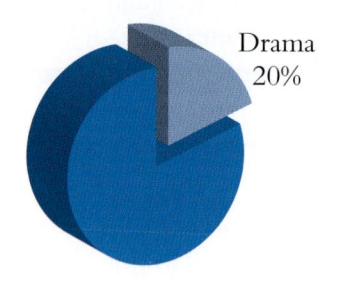

How many marks?
The Drama question (Unit 2: Section A) is worth 20 per cent of the available marks towards your final English Literature grade.

'Quality of written communication'
This is assessed in all units of the examination. You should take care to:
- choose an appropriate form and style for your answer
- organise your material clearly and coherently (e.g. taking care with punctuation and paragraphing)
- write legibly and accurately.

The use of quotation
This is an 'open-book' section and the use of quotation is expected. However, remember that you have only 45 minutes for this question and cannot afford to waste time searching for that half-remembered quotation.

Here are some useful tips:

- Quotation is certainly one way of demonstrating your knowledge of the text, but it is not the only way. **Accurate** and **well selected** reference to the text can help develop your argument and support your ideas.
- Use quotations to make, illustrate or back up a point. Don't waste time by using them to repeat a point, or simply because you have learnt them!
- Try to make your quotations accurate – though the examiner will be realistic.
- Present quotations in inverted commas.
- If the quotation cannot stand alone, make it fit into the surrounding sentence.
- Quotations should be **brief**, **meaningful** and **relevant**.

Question types

Free-standing essay questions

Note that the **free-standing** essay questions considered here are **(a)** questions.

Foundation tier and Higher tier questions

The questions at Foundation tier have bullet points to help you structure your argument. Here are examples of a Foundation tier question and a Higher tier question (on *Blood Brothers*) for comparison.

> **F** (a) Show that Mickey **makes mistakes** in his life.
>
> In your answer you should consider the language and dramatic techniques used in **presenting**:
>
> - Mickey's actions before he goes to jail
> - Mickey's actions after he is released from jail.

> **H** (a) With reference to the ways Russell **presents** Mickey, show how far you agree that Mickey is **responsible** for the things that go wrong in his life.

Unpacking the questions

Both of the questions above use some key terms which are there to guide you and help you to focus your ideas. These terms are in bold to bring them to your attention. For example:

- **makes mistakes** or **responsible** helps you to organise the material and focus your argument
- **presenting** or **presents** reminds you that you must deal with the dramatist's intentions and techniques.

You may have noted that there is a slight difference in the instruction words. At Foundation tier the question asks you to 'show that', so you will be bringing together the evidence to prove that Mickey makes mistakes.

Examiner's tip!

Remember – you are not being asked to write everything you know about the character! Your answer **must focus** on the key terms of the question.

However, at Higher tier the instruction 'show how far you agree that' asks you go that bit further. You may be agreeing, disagreeing, or partly agreeing that Mickey is responsible for the things that go wrong in his life. At both Foundation tier and Higher tier the word 'show' means that you must provide **evidence** for your opinions.

At Foundation tier, the bullet points suggest not only the areas of the play to look at, but also a helpful order in which to consider them. This gives you some support in constructing an argument in response to the question. At Higher tier, you are expected to build a coherent argument based on the key terms of the question. This is why it is so important to spend some time planning your answer before making a start.

Extract-based questions

The **extract-based** questions considered here are **(b)** questions, though you may get an extract-based question as either **(a)** or **(b)**.

Foundation tier and Higher tier questions

The questions at Foundation tier have bullet points to help you structure your argument.

Here are examples of a Foundation tier question and a Higher tier question (on *Blood Brothers*) for comparison.

> **F (b)** Look again at the extract on page 49 beginning with the stage direction *Mrs Johnstone appears, clutching a letter* and ending at the end of Act 1.
>
> Show that Mrs Johnstone's dreams of happiness only provide a **brief escape** from unhappiness.
>
> In your answer you should consider:
>
> - what Mrs Johnstone says in the extract
> - Russell's use of language and dramatic techniques in the extract
> - Mrs Johnstone's dreams of happiness elsewhere in Act 1.

> **H (b)** Look again at the extract on page 49 beginning with the stage direction *Mrs Johnstone appears, clutching a letter* and ending at the end of Act 1.
>
> With reference to the ways Russell **presents** dreams of happiness in the extract and elsewhere in Act 1, show how far you agree that there is **no escape** from unhappiness for the Johnstone family.

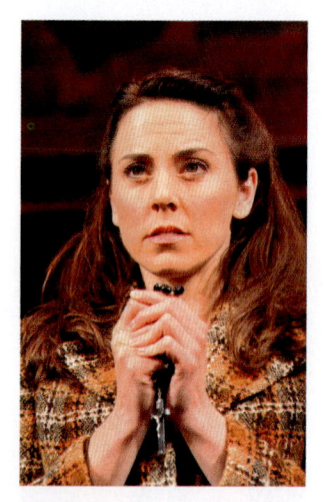

Unpacking the questions

To produce a good answer you must pay attention to the key terms:

- **brief escape** or **no escape** helps you to organise the material and focus your argument

Mrs Johnstone

- the second bullet point at Foundation tier or **presents** at Higher tier reminds you that you must deal with the dramatist's intentions and techniques.

Again, there is a slight difference in the instruction words. At Foundation tier, the words 'show that' mean you will be demonstrating that Mrs Johnstone's dreams of happiness provide only a brief escape from unhappiness. At Higher tier, the words 'show how far you agree that' mean you may be agreeing, disagreeing, or partly agreeing that there is no escape from unhappiness for the Johnstone family. At both Foundation tier and Higher tier the word 'show' means that you must provide **evidence** for your opinions.

As with the free-standing question, at Foundation tier the bullet points suggest not only the areas of the play to look at, but also a helpful order in which to consider them. At Higher tier, you are given more freedom as it is up to you to select which references to the text will help you to construct your argument. Although you have an extract to give you a starting point, planning will be very important. Jot down points which are relevant, then sort these points into a coherent order which you can develop in your answer. Avoid writing a very general essay – to 'score big' you have to focus on the key terms.

How your work is marked

The examiner will be looking for certain key features in your answer:

- **Focus** – Has your response answered the question?
- **Development** – Have you gone into detail?
- **Argument** – Is your response logical and persuasive?
- **Understanding** – Does it show understanding of use of language, characters, events and staging.

These are what you must produce in your answer to ensure success.

Assessment Objectives (AOs)

In this Drama unit (Unit 2: Section A), you need to cover the following AOs and demonstrate that you can:

- **AO1** Respond to texts critically and imaginatively; select and evaluate relevant textual detail to illustrate and support interpretations.
- **AO2** Explain how language, structure and form contribute to writers' presentation of ideas, themes and settings.

Dancing at Lughnasa by Brian Friel

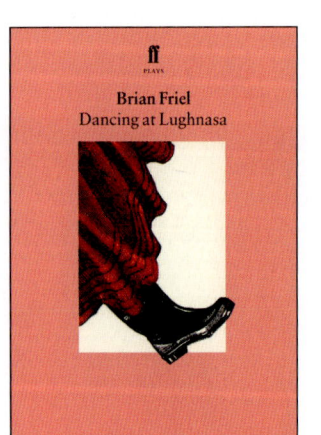

You will find the Mark Schemes for these questions on the CCEA website (www.ccea.org.uk).

Let's look at an extract-based question.

> **H** Look again at the extract from Act 1, beginning near the bottom of page 2 with the stage directions *The lighting changes* and ending on page 6 with the stage directions *Rose closes the front of her apron. She is on the point of tears. Silence.*
>
> With reference to the ways Friel **presents** the Mundy sisters in the extract and elsewhere in the play, show how far you agree that they show **care and concern** for one another.

Here is part of a Band 2 response to this question:

> The Mundy sisters show concern for Rose. Rose is disabled and gets confused easily like when she is talking to Maggie about Africa. I think the sisters try to look after Rose. In the extract, Maggie dances with Rose and holds her hand which it says in the stage directions.

Attempts to focus on key term **concern**.

Aware of stage directions but needs to explain effect.

This is a limited response, which shows a little awareness of what is happening in the extract.

⚠ Think carefully! What could you do to answer this question more successfully? For example:

- Plan your answer – think about how each sister shows care and concern for the others.
- How does the dramatist create the scene – what dramatic techniques does he use?
- Develop ideas – make comments on characters and their actions.

A Band 4 response looks more explicitly at the writer's use of techniques. Here is an extract from a Band 4 response:

> Friel presents the Mundy sisters in ways that show they show care and concern for each other. In the extract, Rose's confusion is evident in the stage direction 'unhappily' but Maggie shows her care for Rose by distracting her 'Maggie catches her hand and sings softly into her ear...' The fact that she sings 'softly' shows her care for Rose.

This response specifically addresses the dramatic techniques Friel uses and comments on their effects.

Examiner's tip!

Use the extract. **Discuss** the techniques the dramatist uses to create the scene.

ACTIVITY 42
Answering an extract-based question

1. Look carefully at the extract and the sample responses. Add more detail to the response by analysing the extract in detail.
2. Now, bring it all together and answer the question.

Now, let's consider a free-standing essay question.

> **H** With reference to the ways Friel **presents** Gerry Evans, show how far you would agree that Gerry Evans is **unreliable**.

A Band 3 response to this question will begin to focus on the key term **unreliable**, for example:

*Begins to address key term **unreliable**.*

> Gerry Evans is unreliable because he left Chris to bring up their child on her own. He only appears every now and again and makes promises that he doesn't keep. This is shown when he says he will buy Michael a bicycle. Chris and Michael are sure that he has got the bike but it never arrives. 'And each time he proposed to Mother and promised me a new bike . . . his visit became more infrequent; and finally he stopped coming altogether.' Michael says this in one of his monologues and this shows that Michael knew that his father let him down.

Comment on character.

Brief comment on dramatic technique.

This student is thinking about the character of Gerry Evans and has selected some relevant information from the text to support the point being made. To improve they should:

- Bring the dramatist into it – refer to the ways Friel presents Gerry Evans as being unreliable. The first sentence could then read 'Friel presents Gerry Evans as unreliable by showing that he left Chris. . .'.
- Bring the response back to the key term – the final sentence could read '. . . the audience understands that Michael knew that his father was unreliable.'
- Consider the way Gerry Evans speaks and acts – think about his exaggeration and boasting.
- Consider if there is any evidence showing that Gerry Evans is not completely unreliable.
- Consider how the sisters react to Gerry, especially Kate and Agnes. How do these reactions show that Gerry Evans is unreliable?

ACTIVITY 43

Answering a free-standing essay question

1 Look at the points listed. Think carefully about each one and select evidence from the text to develop each one in detail.
2 Now, bring it all together and answer the question.

Examiner's tip!

Although there is no bullet point guiding you towards dramatic technique in the question, it is important to address the key term **presents** and discuss the techniques in the play. Consider stage directions, language, tone, use of punctuation (e.g. pauses or hesitation) and structure.

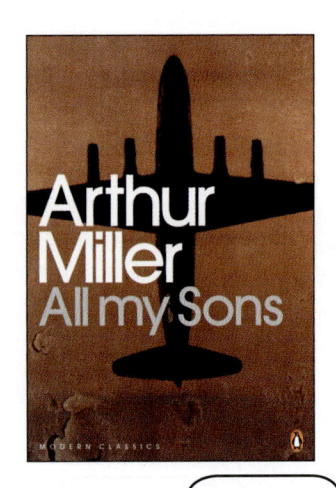

All My Sons by Arthur Miller

You will find the Mark Schemes for these questions on the CCEA website (www.ccea.org.uk).

Let's apply your skills to a free-standing essay question.

> **H** With reference to the ways Miller **presents** Kate, show how far you agree that Kate may be **both pitied and disliked**.

A Band 2 answer will often be like a general character study with only occasional attempts to address the key terms of the question, for example:

Aware of character.

Makes general statements.

> Kate Keller is married to Joe and has lost her son Larry in the war but won't accept that he is dead. She isn't very well and suffers from bad headaches. She is quite rude to Ann, like when she says she has put on weight.

This is a limited, general response.

! Think carefully! What could you do to answer this question more successfully? For example:

- Plan your answer and focus on the key terms – why is Kate pitied? Why can Kate be disliked?
- How does Miller develop her character? What techniques are used?

A Band 4 response will present an argument which considers both aspects of the question, for example:

Focuses on key terms.

Comments on dramatic technique.

Supports ideas with relevant quotation.

> Kate Keller deserves pity because she has lost her son in the war and cannot accept that he is dead. She clings to the hope that he will return – 'Only last week a man turned up in Detroit, missing longer than Larry.' Her desperation is shown by Miller's use of ellipses to show her broken speech. '...Just don't stop believing...'
>
> However Kate can also be disliked because of her belief that Larry will come home because the rest of the family, especially Chris, have to tiptoe round her and keep their own lives on hold. 'You marry that girl and you're pronouncing him dead. Now what's going to happen to Mother?'

This response addresses the key terms and is starting to present an argument, selecting relevant references to the text to develop the discussion. Consider these questions:

- How does Kate treat George and Ann? Is her behaviour towards these characters dislikeable or pitiable?
- Does her protection of Joe make her someone to pity or dislike?
- What is there in her behaviour that makes her pitiable?

ACTIVITY 44

Answering a free-standing essay question

1. Look carefully at the sample responses and points (opposite).
2. Now, bring it all together and answer the question.

Examiner's tip!

Although there is no bullet point guiding you towards dramatic technique in the question, it is important to address the key term **presents** and discuss the techniques in the play. Consider stage directions, language, tone, use of punctuation (e.g. pauses or hesitation) and structure.

Now, let's look at an extract-based question.

> H Look again at the extract in Act 2 beginning on page 65 with Chris's words, 'What do you mean, you packed her bag?' and ending on page 68 with Keller's words, 'For you, a business for you!'
>
> With reference to the ways Miller **presents** Joe and Kate in the extract, and Chris elsewhere in the play, show how far you would agree that their lives are **based on dishonesty**.

Let's consider a sample from a Band 3 response:

> In the extract, both Kate and Joe are being dishonest because they have hidden the truth about what happened at the factory. Kate has been dishonest because she wants to protect the family but also because she doesn't want to admit that Larry is dead. The short sentences build up tension as the truth starts to come out and we can see the lives they have built start to fall apart.

Some focus on key terms.

Comments on dramatic technique.

This response repeats the key term **dishonest** and comments on how the characters' lives are based on dishonesty. How could you answer the question more successfully? For example:

- Examine the extract in detail – what techniques does Miller use to show the characters' dishonesty? Think about how he builds tension in the scene as the truth is revealed.
- Consider each character referred to in the question – what do we learn about Kate and Joe's dishonesty in the extract? What about Chris – how is he dishonest?

Remember, a Band 4 response will develop ideas fully and **discuss** the effects of the techniques the dramatist uses.

ACTIVITY 45

Answering an extract-based question

1. Look at the points above. Select evidence from the text to develop each point in detail.
2. Now, bring it all together and answer the question.

Examiner's tip!

Use the extract. **Discuss** the techniques the dramatist uses to create the scene.

77

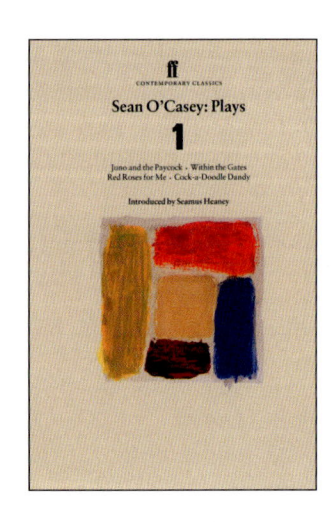

Juno and the Paycock by Sean O'Casey

You will find the Mark Schemes for these questions on the CCEA website (www.ccea.org.uk).

Let's apply your skills to a free-standing essay question.

> **H** With reference to the ways O'Casey **presents** Mrs Madigan, show how far you agree that Mrs Madigan is **motivated** by self-interest.

A Band 2 response will be basic, usually just giving a broad character sketch, for example:

> Mrs Madigan lends Boyle money and is angry when he doesn't repay the loan. She takes away their gramophone even though Boyle tells her it hasn't been paid for, so she is only interested in getting her money back.

Describes what happens.

Hints at key terms of question.

This is a straightforward, descriptive response which shows awareness of what happens in the play and Mrs Madigan's actions.

⚠ Think carefully! What could you do to answer the question more successfully? Consider these questions:

- How does Mrs Madigan speak to Boyle? What does this tell you about her character?
- Why does she lend Boyle money in the first place? Is she acting out of self-interest?
- How does she treat Juno?

A Band 4 response will explicitly discuss writer's techniques and their effects, for example:

> In Act 3, Mrs Madigan demands that Boyle repays the loan. The stage directions say that she speaks 'ominously' which shows that she is intent on getting her money back, even though she is aware that Boyle can't afford it. We can see that she is only thinking about her own self interest here, especially when she 'catches up the gramophone' and takes it to the pawn shop. She mocks Boyle's boasting – 'You're not goin' to be swankin' it like a paycock with Maisie Madigan's money – I'll pull some o' th' gorgeous feathers out o' your tail!' She seems to enjoy this, although it could be argued that it is her money so she deserves to be repaid, especially when it becomes clear that Boyle isn't getting the big inheritance.

Discusses use of language and dramatic technique.

Focuses on key term of question.

This student looks at dramatic techniques like stage directions and goes on to comment on the effect which these techniques create. How would you develop this response? Consider:

- How does Mrs Madigan behave towards other characters in the play? Think about her interactions with Boyle, Juno and Mary.
- Is there a counter argument? Does she behave in an unselfish way towards any characters?
- Bring the dramatist into it – use O'Casey's name when you are discussing how Mrs Madigan speaks and behaves?

Now, let's look at an extract-based question.

> **H** Look again at the extract in Act 2 beginning with the stage direction *Steps are heard approaching, and Juno, opening the door, allows Bentham to enter* and ending with Bentham's words, 'Oh, I'm very sorry, Mrs Boyle; I never thought . . .'.
>
> With reference to the ways O'Casey **presents** Bentham in the extract, and other characters elsewhere in the play, show how far you agree that their attitudes to the Boyle family **change** when they think the Boyles have come into money.

This Band 3 response clearly addresses the key terms of the question:

> O'Casey shows a change in Bentham's attitude to the Boyle family in this extract because he is polite to them and shows an interest in Mary. 'Oh, good evening, Mary; how pretty you're looking!' This tells us that now they have money, he would be happy to marry Mary. He is shown to speak pleasantly to Juno and even appears interested in Boyle's opinions. 'It's just as you were saying, Mr Boyle . . .'

Focuses on key term.

Comments on dramatic technique.

This student has started to consider dramatic technique by commenting on the dramatist's use of dialogue and what this tells us about character. How could this response be developed? For example:

- Analyse the extract – develop the discussion of how O'Casey shows Bentham's attitude towards the Boyles.
- What about elsewhere in the play? Which characters change their attitudes to the family? You could discuss Joxer, Needle Nugent and Mrs Madigan.
- Bring the dramatist into it. Refer explicitly to O'Casey's techniques, e.g. 'O'Casey shows how attitudes to the Boyle family change by . . .'.

ACTIVITY 46
Answering a free-standing essay question

1 Look carefully at the sample responses and points (left). Plan your answer carefully.
2 Now, bring it all together and answer the question.

Examiner's tip!

Use the extract. **Discuss** the techniques the dramatist uses to create the scene.

ACTIVITY 47
Answering an extract-based question

1 Look at the points above. Select evidence from the text to develop each point in detail.
2 Now, bring it all together and answer the question.

An Inspector Calls by J.B. Priestley

You will find the Mark Schemes for these questions on the CCEA website (www.ccea.org.uk).

Let's apply your skills to an extract-based question.

> **H** Look again at the extract beginning on page 51 with the Inspector's words, 'When did you first meet this girl?' and ending on page 53 with Eric's words, 'I got it – from the office. . .'.
>
> With reference to the ways Priestley **presents** Eric in the extract and Eric and Sheila elsewhere in the play, show how far you agree that the behaviour of Eric and Sheila to Eva/Daisy was **selfish**. Do you have any sympathy for Eric and Sheila? Give reasons for your opinions.

Examiner's tip!
There seems to be a lot to this question. Read the extract carefully and focus on the key terms.

Here is part of a Band 2 response:

Attempts to focus on key term.

> I think Eric is selfish because he used Eva. He is not very nice because he gets drunk and sleeps with her even though she tried to stop him. It says he 'threatened to make a row'. I think Sheila is selfish too because she got Eva/Daisy fired from her job just because she looked pretty.

Describes what happens without comment.

This response shows **awareness** of characters and what happens but doesn't go into any detail. However, there is some attempt to consider both Eric and Sheila.

Examiner's tip!
Use the extract. **Discuss** the techniques the dramatist uses to create the scene.

> **!** Think carefully! What could you do to answer this question more successfully? Consider these suggestions:
>
> - Examine what Eric says in the extract – is he completely selfish or does he show some consideration for Eva/Daisy?
> - Give evidence to support the statement about Sheila being 'selfish too'.
> - Explain your opinions about Eric and Sheila – can you feel sympathy for them?

ACTIVITY 48
Answering an extract-based question

1. Look carefully at the points above. Select evidence from the text to develop each point in detail.
2. Now, bring it all together and answer the question.

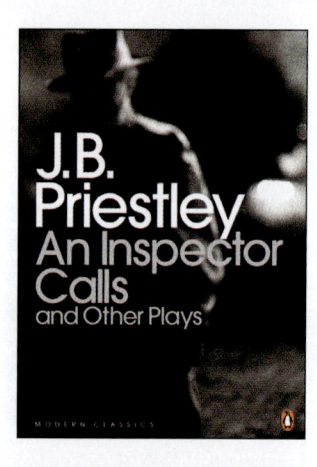

Now, let's consider a free-standing essay question.

> **H** With reference to the ways Priestley **presents** Gerald Croft, show that Gerald is **sometimes selfish and sometimes thoughtful** in his relationships with Sheila and Eva/Daisy.

This question is guiding you to present an argument by looking at **two** aspects of Gerald's interactions with Sheila and Eva/Daisy. Here is part of a Band 2 response:

> Gerald Croft doesn't think about his girlfriend Sheila when he has an affair with Daisy so he is selfish. He is selfish to Daisy as well because when they break up he doesn't really think about her or even know where she went. But he did give her some money which is thoughtful.

Straightforward – gives some information but no detail.

Draws some basic conclusions which could be explored.

⚠️ Think carefully! What could you do to answer this question more successfully? For example:

- Plan your answer – think about Gerald and Sheila then Gerald and Eva/Daisy. How is his behaviour selfish or thoughtful?
- How does Priestley use dramatic techniques to develop Gerald's character? Consider the way he speaks about Daisy and Sheila.

A Band 4 response brings the dramatist into consideration, for example:

> Priestley shows us that Gerald is sometimes thoughtful towards Daisy in the way he speaks about her. He describes her affectionately as being 'young, pretty and warm-hearted...' which encourages our sympathy a little and shows that Gerald had some affection for her. He also treated her thoughtfully when he 'rescued' her from Joe Meggarty. However, he is shown to be quite selfish because while he was thoughtfully organising somewhere for Daisy to live and giving her money so that she could survive, he exploited her gratitude and had an affair with her because it made him feel like 'the wonderful Fairy Prince'.

Comments on use of language.

*Develops an argument, focused on key terms **selfish** and **thoughtful**.*

Interprets character and actions.

This response is beginning to show more detailed consideration of the key terms of the question.

ACTIVITY 49

Answering a free-standing essay question

1. Consider Gerald's treatment of Sheila. In what ways is Gerald shown to treat her thoughtfully or selfishly? Write a paragraph for each, supporting your points with relevant evidence from the text.
2. Now, bring it all together and answer the question.

Examiner's tip!

Although there is no bullet point guiding you towards dramatic technique in the question, it is important to address the key term **presents** and discuss the techniques the dramatist uses in the play. Consider stage directions, language, tone, use of punctuation (e.g. pauses or hesitation) and structure.

Blood Brothers by Willy Russell

You will find the Mark Schemes for these questions on the CCEA website (www.ccea.org.uk).

Let's apply your skills to an extract-based question.

> **H** Look at the extract beginning with the stage direction *Mrs Johnstone appears, clutching a letter* and ending at the end of Act 1.
>
> With reference to the ways Russell **presents** dreams of happiness in the extract and elsewhere in Act 1, show how far you would agree that there is **no escape** from unhappiness for the Johnstone family.

A Band 2 response to this question will be simple and straightforward, for example:

> In this scene Mrs Johnstone and her family are able to get away from where they live and all the neighbours are happy because they are leaving. Mrs Johnstone thinks that she is going to escape and sings about how wonderful life is going to be.

Aware of events but very limited.

*Simple reference to 'escape' but not closely tied into key term **no escape**.*

This example is very limited. The student mentions Mrs Johnstone's song but doesn't take the reference to dramatic technique any farther.

⚠ Think carefully! What could you do to answer this question more successfully? For example:

- Explore the extract in detail – especially the stage directions and the language used in the songs. How do these **dramatic techniques** link with the key terms of the question?
- Select relevant evidence from Act 1. How does Russell show in Act 1 that the Johnstone family can't escape unhappiness?

To move into a higher Mark Band, the answer needs to examine explicitly the techniques the dramatist uses to develop the theme. Here is a sample from a Band 4 response:

> In this extract Russell shows Mrs Johnstone's happiness at moving away in her singing and dancing. Her optimism about the future is shown in the repetition of the words 'Oh bright new day!' which shows that Mrs Johnstone sees this move as a chance to escape the unhappiness of her current situation. 'We're startin' all over again, We're leavin' this mess'.

Comments on writer's technique.

Uses relevant quotation from text to support ideas.

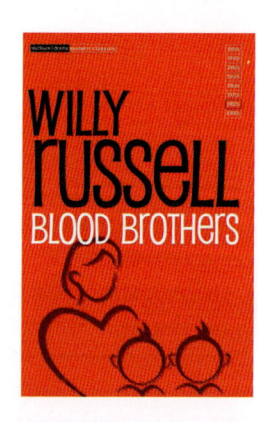

Examiner's tip!

Read the question carefully – you are asked to focus on events in Act 1. Don't waste time looking for evidence from Act 2.

ACTIVITY 50

Answering an extract-based question

1. Continue to examine the extract by selecting relevant information and analysing the effects created.
2. Now, bring it all together and answer the question.

Now, let's look at a free-standing essay question.

> **H** With reference to the ways Russell **presents** Mickey, show how far you would agree that Mickey is **responsible** for the things that go wrong in his life.

A Band 3 response to this question will show some focus on the key terms of the question and attempt to present an argument, for example:

> Mickey is not totally responsible for the things that go wrong in his life. If his mother had been stronger, she wouldn't have split the boys up when they were babies, so to some extent Mrs Johnstone bears some responsibility. Also, Mrs Johnstone can't provide her children with a good life, which means Sammy turns to crime and takes Mickey with him. However, Mickey could have said no to Sammy.

Considers key term of question.

Starts to present an argument in response to key terms.

Comments on characters.

This response is beginning to construct an argument, linked to the key term of the question. To move this into a higher Mark Band, you could:

- Plan the answer – create a concept map to organise ideas in order to build the argument.
- Develop ideas in detail – show your thinking.
- Support ideas with relevant reference to the text.
- Consider how Russell uses dramatic techniques to develop character.

ACTIVITY 51

Answering a free-standing essay question

1. Look again at the points above. Select evidence from the text to develop each point in detail.
2. Now, bring it all together and answer the question.

Examiner's tip!

Although there is no bullet point guiding you towards dramatic technique in the question, it is important to address the key term **presents** and discuss the techniques the dramatist uses in the play. Consider stage directions, language, tone, use of punctuation (e.g. pauses or hesitation) and structure.

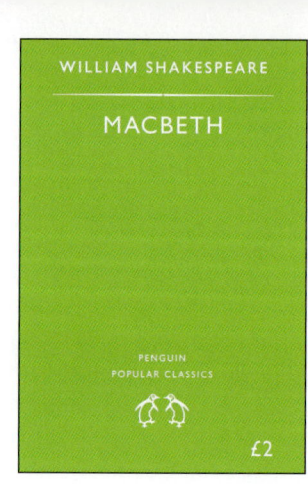

Macbeth by William Shakespeare

You will find the Mark Schemes for these questions on the CCEA website (www.ccea.org.uk).

Let's apply your skills to a free-standing essay question.

> **H** With reference to the ways Shakespeare **presents** Macbeth, show how far you agree that Macbeth is **evil**.

A Band 2 response will be basic, usually just giving a broad character sketch, for example:

Attempts to address key term.

Describes what happens.

> Macbeth is evil because he killed King Duncan even though he was a visitor in his castle. Once he has killed Duncan, he goes on and has his friend Banquo killed as well and murders Lady Macduff and her children.

Think carefully! What could you do to answer this question more successfully? Consider these questions:

- How does Macbeth change through the course of the play?
- What influences his behaviour?
- Does he behave only in an evil way?

A Band 4 response will develop ideas in detail and explicitly discuss the writer's technique, for example:

Discusses use of language and structure.

Focuses on key term.

> At the start of the play, Macbeth is presented as a hero who has fought bravely for his king. 'For brave Macbeth – well he deserves that name...' Everyone praises his courage and he is honoured by Duncan for his bravery. However, by the end of the play he is described as 'this dead butcher' and we have to examine what he has done to deserve this name, what has happened to make him carry out such evil acts.

This student looks at how Macbeth is presented through the words used to describe him and makes some comment on the structure of the play. How would you develop this response? For example:

- You are invited to present an argument – do you agree that Macbeth is purely evil or are there other factors which should be taken into account? What are these factors?
- Bring the dramatist into it – how is Macbeth presented? Consider how he struggles with his conscience and how other characters describe him.

ACTIVITY 52

Answering a free-standing essay question

1. Look carefully at the sample responses and points (above). Plan your answer with care.
2. Now, bring it all together and answer the question.

Now, let's look at an extract-based question.

> **H** Look again at Act 1 Scene 3.
>
> With reference to the ways Shakespeare **presents** the witches in this scene, and elsewhere in the play, show how far you agree that the witches are **frightening** and **powerful**.

A Band 3 response to this question will clearly address the key terms of the question, for example:

> The witches in this extract are shown to be frightening by the way Banquo describes them. 'What are these/ So wither'd and so wild in their attire/ That look not like the inhabitants of the earth.' This encourages the audience to imagine strange beings which can be frightening, especially at the time the play was set. They are also shown to be powerful because they seem to be able to change the weather. 'I'll give thee a wind.'

Focuses on key term.

Comments on language.

This response does the right thing – it looks closely at the extract and Shakespeare's use of language, beginning to comment on the effect of the words. How could you develop this response? For example:

- Plan your answer – create a concept map to organise your ideas into a logical order.
- Analyse the extract – how does Shakespeare present the witches? Consider their words and how Banquo and Macbeth react to them.
- Which scenes should you discuss with reference to the witches? How does Shakespeare show that the witches are powerful and frightening elsewhere in the play?
- Bring the dramatist into it. Refer explicitly to his techniques, e.g. 'Shakespeare shows the witches are frightening and powerful by . . .'.

ACTIVITY 53
Answering an extract-based question
1 Look again at the points above. Select evidence from the text to develop each point in detail.
2 Now, bring it all together and answer the question.

Examiner's tip!
Use the extract. **Discuss** the techniques the playwright uses to create the scene.

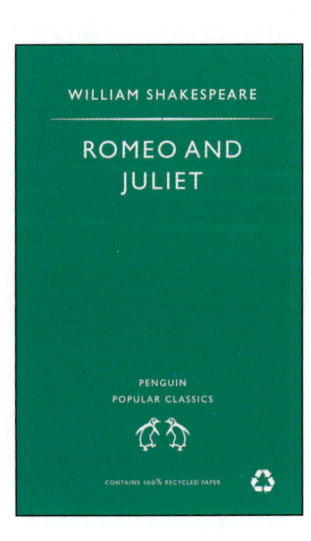

Romeo and Juliet by William Shakespeare

You will find the Mark Schemes for these questions on the CCEA website (www.ccea.org.uk).

Let's apply your skills to a free-standing essay question.

> **H** With reference to the ways Shakespeare **presents** the Nurse, show how far you agree that she is **helpful** to the Capulet family.

A Band 2 response will be very general, often giving a broad character sketch, for example:

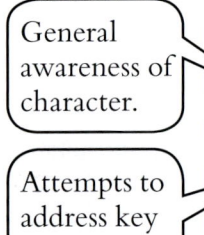

General awareness of character.

*Attempts to address key term **helpful**.*

> The Nurse has worked for the Capulet family for a long time and looks after Juliet. She sorts out Juliet's clothes and puts her to bed at night. She also helps Juliet by carrying messages for her to arrange meetings.

This is a simple answer showing awareness of the Nurse but is too general.

! Think carefully! What could you do to answer this question more successfully? For example:

- Focus on the key terms of the question – how is the Nurse **helpful** to the Capulet family?
- How is the Nurse **presented**? What is there in her speech and behaviour which shows that she is helpful?
- Is there anything in the Nurse's behaviour that shows she is **not** helpful? Consider the whole Capulet family, not just Juliet.

A Band 4 response will develop ideas in detail and construct an argument which is reasoned, with carefully selected reference to the text, for example:

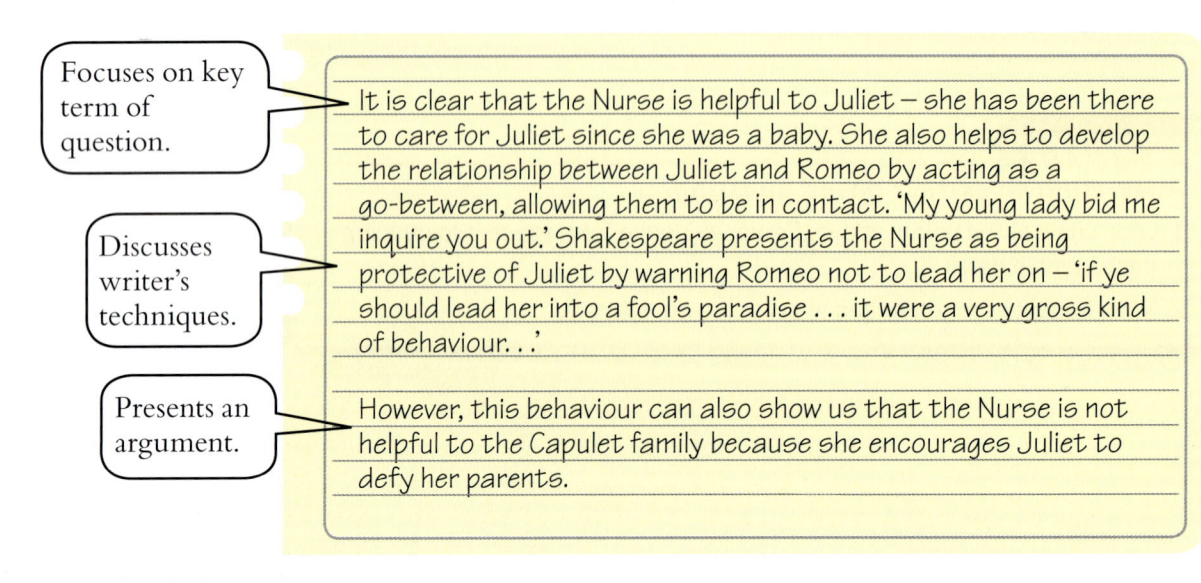

Focuses on key term of question.

Discusses writer's techniques.

Presents an argument.

> It is clear that the Nurse is helpful to Juliet – she has been there to care for Juliet since she was a baby. She also helps to develop the relationship between Juliet and Romeo by acting as a go-between, allowing them to be in contact. 'My young lady bid me inquire you out.' Shakespeare presents the Nurse as being protective of Juliet by warning Romeo not to lead her on – 'if ye should lead her into a fool's paradise . . . it were a very gross kind of behaviour. . .'
>
> However, this behaviour can also show us that the Nurse is not helpful to the Capulet family because she encourages Juliet to defy her parents.

This student focuses on the key terms of the question, especially 'show how far you agree . . .'. What could be done to develop this response? For example:

- How does the Nurse help Juliet and Romeo's relationship to grow?
- What evidence is there from the text to support the argument in the second paragraph in the Band 4 response?
- Are the Nurse's actions helpful, considering the outcome of the play? Develop this idea into an argument.
- Bring the dramatist into it – use Shakespeare's name when you are discussing how the Nurse speaks and behaves.

Now, let's look at an extract-based question.

> **H** Look again at the extract in Act 1 Scene 1, lines 66–106, beginning with Benvolio's words: 'Part, fools! Put up your swords' and ending when Prince Escalus says 'Once more, on pain of death, all men depart.'
>
> With reference to the ways Shakespeare **presents** the feuding between Montagues and Capulets in the extract, show that there are **differing attitudes** to it. To what extent does the Prince bring the feuding under control elsewhere in the play? Give reasons for your opinions.

A Band 3 response to this question will clearly address the key terms of the question, for example:

> In the extract there are some different attitudes to the fighting. [Focuses on key term.] Benvolio tries to stop it 'I drew to part them' while Tybalt is keen to fight – 'What, drawn, and talk of peace? . . . Have at thee, coward!' Here Tybalt mocks Benvolio for wanting peace and calls [Comments on language.] him a coward.

This response is beginning to discuss the key term of the question and make some comment on the use of language. How would you answer this question more successfully? For example:

- Analyse the extract – how does Shakespeare show differing attitudes to the feuding? Discuss the dialogue – the commands and exclamations and their effect.
- What about elsewhere in the play? Do the Prince's interventions have any effect? Do any characters show a change in their attitudes to the fighting?
- Bring the dramatist into it. Refer explicitly to Shakespeare's techniques, e.g. 'Shakespeare shows differing attitudes to the feuding by . . .'.

ACTIVITY 54
Answering a free-standing essay question

1. Look carefully at the sample responses and points (left). Plan your answer with care.
2. Now, bring it all together and answer the question.

Examiner's tip!
Read the question carefully – there seems to be a lot to deal with. Focus on the key terms in **bold**.

ACTIVITY 55
Answering an extract-based question

1. Look again at the points above. Select evidence from the text to develop each point in detail.
2. Now, bring it all together and answer the question.

Examiner's tip!
Use the extract. **Discuss** the techniques the playwright uses to create the scene.

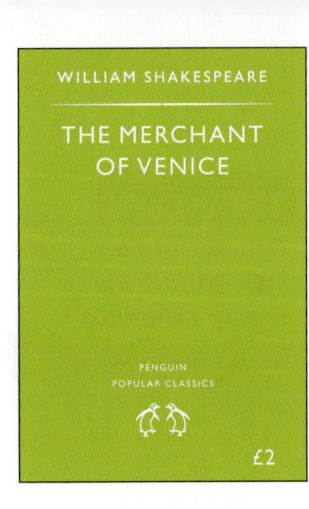

The Merchant of Venice by William Shakespeare

You will find the Mark Schemes for these questions on the CCEA website (www.ccea.org.uk).

Let's apply your skills to a free-standing essay question.

> **H** With reference to the ways Shakespeare **presents** Gratiano, show how far you agree that Gratiano is a **loyal friend** to Bassanio.

Look at this extract from a Band 2 response:

> Gratanio supports his friend Bassanio during the trial and makes fun of Shylock. He is also there when Bassanio gets engaged to Portia and he gets engaged to Nerissa. He is happy to get involved in Bassanio's plans.

(Make sure you spell names correctly!)

*(No explicit link to key term **loyal friend**.)*

This is a limited answer – it shows some awareness of what happens but is too general.

⚠ Think carefully! What could you do to answer this question more successfully? For example:

- Focus on the key terms of the question – how is Gratiano **loyal** to Bassanio?
- How is Gratiano **presented**? What is there in his speech and behaviour that shows that he is a loyal friend?
- Is there anything in Gratiano's behaviour that shows he is **not** a loyal friend?

At Band 4, students will be able to discuss dramatic techniques, for example:

> Shakespeare presents Gratiano as being loud and sometimes thoughtless. For example in Act 2 Scene 2, Bassanio has to warn him about his behaviour before they go to Belmont. 'But hear thee Gratiano/ Thou are too wild, too rude, and bold of voice...' Maybe Bassanio doesn't think that Gratiano is a loyal friend, he seems to think he will embarrass him in front of Portia.
>
> However, Gratiano's loyalty is shown in his outbursts against Shylock and when he copies Bassanio's declaration that he would sacrifice his wife for Antonio. 'I have a wife, whom, I protest, I love:/ I would she were in heaven, so she could /Entreat some power to change this currish Jew.'

(Discusses writer's techniques.)

(Some interpretation.)

(Presents an argument.)

This response is in Band 4 because:

- Focus on the key term **loyal friend** is sustained.
- The student responds to the key term **show how far you agree** and examines whether Gratiano can be called a loyal friend.

- There is explicit reference to writer's technique and the effect created by interpreting Bassanio's interaction with Gratiano.
- There is relevant quotation used to support ideas.

ACTIVITY 56

Answering a free-standing essay question

1. Look carefully at the sample responses and points (on page 88). How would you develop the Band 4 response further? Plan your answer carefully.
2. Now, bring it all together and answer the question.

Now, let's look at an extract-based question.

> Look again at Act 3 Scene 2, line 291 to the end of the scene. (The extract begins with Portia's words 'Is it your dear friend that is thus in trouble?')
>
> With reference to the ways Shakespeare **presents** Portia and Bassanio in the extract and elsewhere in the play, show how far you would agree that they are **loyal** to each other.

Look at this excerpt from a Band 3 response:

> In the extract, Portia shows love and concern for Bassanio when she hears about Antonio's problems. She offers to help – 'You shall have gold/ To pay this petty debt twenty times over' because she doesn't want anyone to be hurt because of Bassanio – 'Before a friend of this description/ Shall lose a hair through Bassanio's fault.' This shows her loyalty because she doesn't question Bassanio – she just supports him.

Comments on character.

*Focuses on key term **loyal**.*

This response is beginning to discuss the key term of the question and comment on characters. How would you answer this question more successfully? For example:

- Plan your answer – create a concept map to organise your ideas into a logical sequence.
- Consider the extract – how does Portia show loyalty to Bassanio? How does Bassanio show loyalty to Portia?
- What about elsewhere in the play? Can you construct a counter argument that there is some disloyalty in the relationship?
- Bring the dramatist into it. Refer explicitly to Shakespeare's techniques, e.g. 'Shakespeare shows Portia's loyalty to Bassanio by . . .'.

ACTIVITY 57

Answering an extract-based question

1. Look again at the points above. Select evidence from the text to develop each point in detail.
2. Now, bring it all together and answer the question.

Examiner's tip!

Use the extract. **Discuss** the techniques the playwright uses to create the scene.

Unit 2

The Study of Drama and Poetry
Section B: Poetry

Introduction

The three Anthologies

The poems in Anthology 1 deal with love and death. In Anthology 2 the themes are nature and war. Some of the poems deal with both themes. You will usually be asked to compare an older poem with a more modern one.

Anthology 3 consists of six poems by Seamus Heaney and six by Thomas Hardy. You will be asked to write about one poem by each poet.

Two types of question may be asked. Either both poems will be named, or one poem will be named and you will be invited to choose a second poem relevant to the question. It is vital that you choose a suitable poem and that you focus carefully on the key terms of the question.

Because of the kinds of question that you will be asked, it is important that you study the twelve poems in your chosen Anthology in detail. This, and careful revision and practice, will enable you to face this section of the examination with confidence.

Explanation of how each Anthology poem is presented in this section

- The pages on each poem begin with a brief paragraph indicating some of the contextual material that may be found useful by students. This information is not complete, of course, and students may wish to research their own.
- This is followed by a set of questions ('Understanding the Poem') designed to explore meaning and specific uses of language in each poem.
- The sample material that comes next is headed 'Moving up the Grades'. It is annotated, and the annotation is based on the Poetry Assessment Grid. The sample material is usually a response to a question which is suggested in brief form. These questions can easily be expanded into the examination paper format and used for class and revision practice.
- Finally, there is a short list of 'Terms for Review' intended to maintain the active use of a critical vocabulary.

Question types

Let's look at a Higher tier question. (As in other units, the Foundation tier questions have bullet points to help you.)

> **H** Look again at 'Thatcher' by Seamus Heaney and at 'The Old Workman' by Thomas Hardy, which both deal with **ideas about work**.
>
> With close reference to the ways each poet uses language, compare and contrast what the speakers in the poems say about **ideas about work**. You should include relevant contextual material.
>
> Which poem do you find more interesting? Give your reasons.

The key term in bold – **ideas about work** – is the focus of this question. You should refer to it frequently in your answer.

This sample question names *both* poems which you must consider. Another type of question names one poem and asks you to choose the second. Make sure you choose carefully!

Unpacking the question

The question above includes these instructions:

- 'With close reference to the ways each poet uses language'
- 'compare and contrast'
- 'include relevant contextual material'
- 'Which poem do you find more interesting? Give your reasons.'

'With close reference to the ways each poet uses language' is asking you to examine the poet's technique – close attention to this will move you up the grades, but remember: what you say must be relevant to the key term – **ideas about work**.

'Compare and contrast' is the main instruction in the question. Look for similarities and differences. And don't forget that this can apply to use of language as well as what the poems are about.

'Include relevant contextual material' is asking you to provide background information – about the work described in the poems, the societies where the workers lived, the poets' own experiences, and so on. Don't forget: it should be relevant to the key term – **ideas about work**.

'Which poem do you find more interesting? Give your reasons.' means the examiner is looking for an explanation of your preference. This part of the question is often left out by students. This provides you with an opportunity to make your answer stand out.

Two new skills

Two new skills are assessed in the Poetry unit (Unit 2: Section A), as well as your knowledge of the poems and of the poets' use of language. These skills are the ability to:

- compare and contrast
- use contextual information.

Comparing and contrasting

Comparing and contrasting means pointing out similarities and differences that are **interesting and significant** between the two poems you are writing about. It is easy to spot and tempting to write about similarities and differences that are not interesting or significant. In a good answer, you need to make sure that what you say is **focused on the question**.

Context

The first thing to remember is that what we are talking about here is **useful and relevant background information**. Some advice:

- Do not give in to the temptation to show off what you know.
- Do not let the contextual information become too prominent or lengthy in your answers. The poems, not the context, are your main concern.

Contextual material can improve and add meaning to your answer. It will not do much to compensate for faulty knowledge or limited understanding of the poems themselves.

Look at this sample opening paragraph. The key term of the question is **work**.

> **Examiner's tip!**
> To move up the grades, try to incorporate the contextual information into your argument, rather than just setting it down as a separate paragraph, unconnected with the argument.

Relevant and useful information about the poet's life.

*Clearly related to key term **work**.*

Irrelevant material. Waste of time!

> In his early poems, Seamus Heaney found popularity when he wrote about his childhood on the family farm in the 1940s. Even then the trade of thatcher was passing away as Ulster modernised. When we consider 'Thatcher' as a poem about work, we are looking at work which is old-fashioned and a little mysterious, and which might draw an interested crowd to see how it was done. This seems to happen in the poem where the spectators are left 'gasping at his Midas touch'.
>
> Thomas Hardy's poem about work, 'The Old Workman' is also based in the poet's childhood. Hardy's father was a stone-mason and as a child Hardy may have met old stone-workers like the one he describes. Later in life Hardy became a famous novelist. He wrote most of his best known poems after he stopped writing novels, when he was an old man.

This student makes some relevant comments about the poets' background; however additional, irrelevant material adds nothing to the understanding of the poems and earns no credit. Be selective with context.

Choosing a second poem

If both poems are named in the question you have no worry here. If only one poem is named you have both an opportunity and a danger: an opportunity to write about a poem you like, but a danger that you will choose a poem because you like it (or know it), but which is not suitable for answering the question. Don't go into the examination with poems so firmly paired in your mind that you cannot be flexible. Read the question, consider the key terms printed in bold, and make sure that the poems you choose to write on are suited to these key terms.

Areas that might give you opportunities for comparing and contrasting are:

- subject matter or theme
- tone
- the speaker
- style.

Subject matter or theme

The poems in each Anthology are grouped around certain themes – for example love; death; war; nature; work; childhood and age. You can expect questions to be directed towards these themes, but make sure you read the key terms of the question carefully. There are many questions that could be asked about each of these themes.

Tone

The poet's attitude towards their subject may be conveyed through tone. For example, the cool, fatalistic tone in Yeats's 'An Irish Airman Foresees His Death' is very different from the shocked tone of Sassoon's 'Attack'. Yet, both poems are about war. Poets may write about the same theme using very different tones, and conveying very different attitudes. (Or the tone within a poem may shift, revealing a change in attitude.)

> **ACTIVITY 1**
>
> **Tone**
>
> Identify two poems in your Anthology which deal with similar themes. Write a few sentences in which you compare and contrast the tone or tones used by each poet. Back up what you say with quotation.

The speaker

At Foundation tier the words 'the speaker' appear in the question, but at Higher tier there is no reminder. You need to be aware that poets may choose to express themselves through a speaker. In other poems the poet may seem to be speaking in their own voice. Sometimes you can make a useful comparison or contrast by considering the speaker of the poem.

ACTIVITY 2

The speaker

Compare and contrast the effect that using a speaker has on the meaning of one of these pairs of poems:

- 'La Belle Dame sans Merci' and 'Piazza Piece'
- 'The Attack' and 'In Westminster Abbey'
- 'Blackberry Picking' and 'An August Midnight'.

Style

There are many aspects of style that you may wish to consider – the use of imagery, sound effects such as rhyme or alliteration, verse forms, syntax or punctuation. Useful comparisons and contrasts can be made but you should always try to say what the **effects** of these stylistic features may be, and how they relate to the key term of the question.

Here is part of a Band 2 response. The key term of the question was **differing attitudes to nature**.

This student has some ideas about the poems but does not develop the points or connect them to the key term of the question: **differing attitudes to nature**. If you want to move up the Mark Bands, you must pay attention to the key terms.

Notices relevant features of poets' style and compares them at a basic level.

Makes only very simple connections between poems.

> Emily Dickinson in 'A narrow fellow in the grass' uses a metaphor for the snake, 'a spotted shaft' and later another metaphor 'a Whip lash'.
>
> Wordsworth uses metaphors too in 'Westminster Bridge' when he calls London a 'mighty heart'.
>
> Dickinson has very unusual punctuation with capital letters in the wrong places and lots of dashes. However Wordsworth's punctuation is normal.

Here is part of a Band 4/5 response. This student notices exactly the same things but uses the material more profitably:

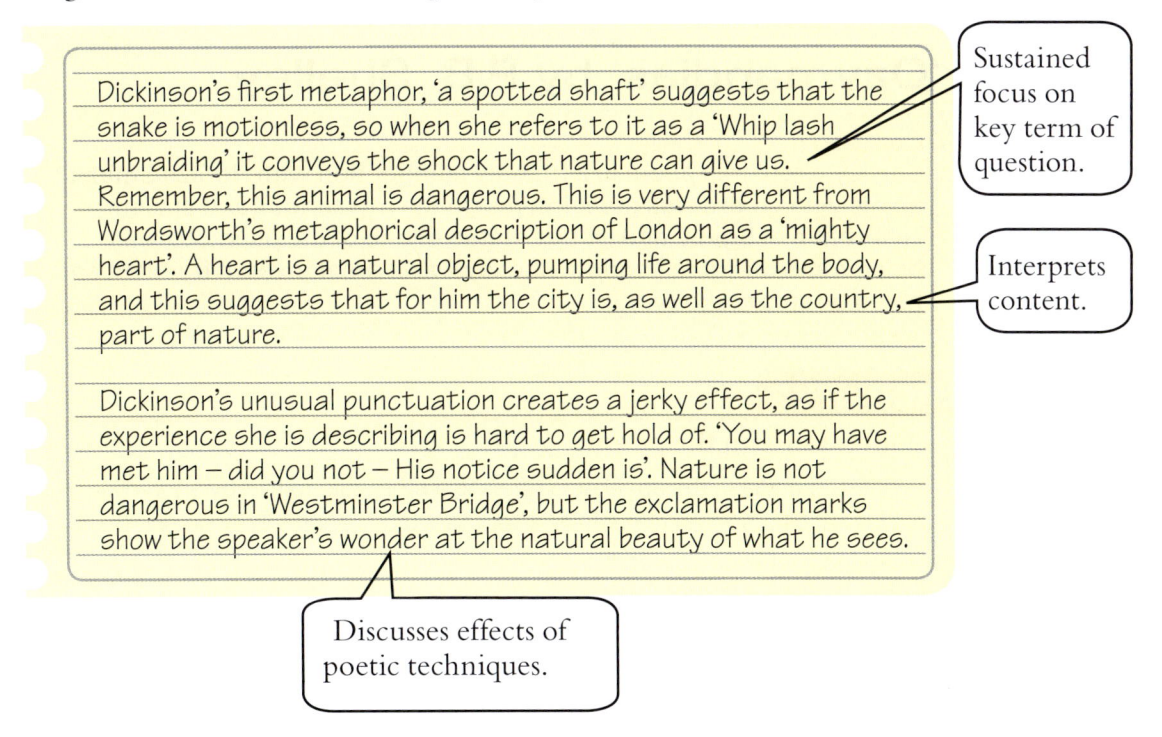

> Dickinson's first metaphor, 'a spotted shaft' suggests that the snake is motionless, so when she refers to it as a 'Whip lash unbraiding' it conveys the shock that nature can give us. Remember, this animal is dangerous. This is very different from Wordsworth's metaphorical description of London as a 'mighty heart'. A heart is a natural object, pumping life around the body, and this suggests that for him the city is, as well as the country, part of nature.
>
> Dickinson's unusual punctuation creates a jerky effect, as if the experience she is describing is hard to get hold of. 'You may have met him – did you not – His notice sudden is'. Nature is not dangerous in 'Westminster Bridge', but the exclamation marks show the speaker's wonder at the natural beauty of what he sees.

Annotations: Sustained focus on key term of question. Interprets content. Discusses effects of poetic techniques.

This student responds to opportunities to compare and contrast, although this could be developed a little further when dealing with punctuation.

Planning your answer

Very basic answers will not compare or contrast at all, or will include only simple remarks, usually at the end, when the student answers the part of the question that asks which poem is more effective, or which poem they prefer.

Many students are too ambitious and try from the start to deal with both poems at once. Be careful – this can result in an awkward 'ping-pong' effect, making it hard to develop your ideas. You might be better dealing with one poem first, and then, while you are dealing with the second poem, you can refer back to the first one and make your comparisons and contrasts. Find a method that works for you.

Anthology 1: Love and Death

'Ozymandias' by P.B. Shelley

Context
Shelley wrote this poem in a friendly competition with Horace Smith at a time when there was great interest in the mysterious and ancient civilisation of Egypt, and a huge statue of one of the pharaohs was being transported to London. Shelley was a great lover of freedom and hated tyrants and tyranny.

ACTIVITY 3

Understanding the poem

1. In 'Ozymandias', the speaker is retelling a story told to him by a traveller. The traveller seems to hesitate after the word 'desert'. Why do you think Shelley makes him hesitate?
2. What words are used to suggest the state of the broken statue in lines 2 and 4?
3. What impression of Ozymandias emerges from the description of his face in lines 4 and 5?
4. Line 8 is a little puzzling. Whose was 'the hand that mocked him'? What do you think this line is hinting at?
5. In the **sestet** the poet turns to the inscription on the base of the statue. Why do you think Ozymandias had these words written? Why does the poet keep this detail back until the second part of the poem?
6. At the end of the poem the traveller seems to turn away from the statue. What does he see, and why does Shelley end the poem in this way?
7. What, for you, is the most memorable image in the poem? Give reasons for your choice.

Moving up the grades

For these responses, the key term of the question was **death**. This is not the only question that could be asked on this poem. Read the question on your examination paper carefully.

Look again at 'Ozymandias' by P.B. Shelley which deals with the theme of **death** . . .

> Mentions key term 'death' but should mention it again at the end of the paragraph.

> Mentions poetic technique but does not do much with it. What has the alliteration to do with the key term 'death'?

> The sestet of the poem brings home the theme of death again, this time it is the death of Ozymandias. The inscription tells us his boastful title is 'King of Kings' and the destruction of his statue is told in a short sentence which gives it emphasis: 'Nothing beside remains.' The alliteration of b and l in the last two lines also adds to the effect.

> The sestet of the poem brings home the theme of death again, this time it is the death of Ozymandias. The inscription tells us his boastful title is 'King of Kings' and the destruction of his statue is told in a short sentence which gives it emphasis: 'Nothing beside remains.' The alliteration of b and l in the last two lines also adds to the effect.

Picks up tone, 'boastful'.

Mentions poetic technique but does not do much with it. What has the alliteration to do with the key term?

This is a Band 3 response with some focus on the question. It comments on some features of the poem, using the correct terms. It begins to develop ideas but there are certainly some areas that could be developed further.

> The sestet of 'Ozymandias' turns from the statue and its sneering face to the pedestal, and the death theme becomes much clearer. The cruelty and arrogance of the king is conveyed in the way the inscription is worded, with the word 'despair' being emphasised by falling at the end of a line. He commanded his enemies to despair but death has overtaken him. The poem ends with the message that 'Nothing beside remains', emphasised by the full-stop. Death is final. There is a last look round the empty desert landscape – death and destruction have left nothing.
>
> The phrase 'colossal wreck' sums up the death of Ozymandias's hopes and dreams and we can hear the winds blowing over the sands in 'sands stretch'. This clever use of sound effects ends the poem with an image of the wreckage of the statue of a dead king in a dead landscape.

Sustained focus – keeps key term in mind throughout.

Ideas are developed.

Some discussion of effects of structure and poetic techniques.

This is a good Band 4 response. The student shows determination to stay relevant, and focuses on the key term **death** throughout. Ideas are developed clearly and, importantly, the poetic techniques are not identified for their own sake, but related to the question.

Review

Let's review some of the key words and ideas for this poem:

- **sonnet**
- **octave**
- **sestet**
- **alliteration**.

Make sure you understand each term clearly. Make a list of definitions which you can use for revision.

'A Poison Tree' by William Blake

> **Context**
> Blake seems to have believed that an impulse of feeling should not be suppressed as this could lead to it changing into a dangerous hatred. In this poem he speaks of the need to express our impulses of anger, even to those we love: better to express the anger – 'talk things through' – and get it out of the way. (With these ideas Blake could be difficult company.) He puts forward this idea in several of his poems. Do you agree with it? Have you ever used the phrase 'clearing the air'? What does it mean?

ACTIVITY 4

Understanding the poem

1. In the course of the poem the **extended image** of the tree comes to be used for the speaker's anger. At what point does his anger 'become' a tree and what words in the poem refer to the 'anger-tree'? (Look at the paragraph on symbols on page 24.)
2. What is the key difference between the speaker's treatment of his friend and his enemy in the first **quatrain**?
3. The second quatrain deals with two differing kinds of behaviour. What kinds of behaviour is the angry speaker describing? Can you argue that, fundamentally, the two kinds of behaviour are similar?
4. What do you think the apple in the third quatrain symbolises?
5. This poem is written in a very simple style. There are simple one-syllable rhymes (sometimes called masculine rhymes) and a lot of repetition. What are the effects of this? (The Band 4 sample below gives a possible response.)
6. What do you think Blake wants us to think of the speaker in the poem? Look particularly at the fourth quatrain. Give reasons for your opinions.

Moving up the grades

This response deals with the style of the poem. The question was about the theme of **strong emotions for another person**.

> As Blake writes about the strong hatred he has for his enemy, there is much repetition of the words 'I' and 'my' in the poem, especially in the first verse where the repetition is used together with contrast ('friend'/'foe', 'end'/'grow') to show two situations in very few words. Another word which is repeated is 'and'. This gives the impression of a story being told very simply, without explanation.

This is from a lower Band 4 response. It comments on poetic techniques (**repetition**, **contrast**), and begins to say something about the **effects** of the techniques. It is a pity that the student does not say more about that interesting final point.

We looked at **symbolism** in the 'Language and style' section of the Prose unit (page 24). The advantage of symbolism for a poet especially is that a symbol can say a lot in a few words. As in this poem, a simple object can stand for a set of ideas:

> In the morning glad I see
> My foe outstretch'd beneath the tree.

Key Word

Symbol
An object which the writer makes stand for something else

This is a poem where you need to pay attention to the **speaker**. It may be that Blake is confessing to us that he was overjoyed to see his enemy dead beneath a tree – or that may not be the case at all! Probably Blake uses a first-person speaker to make the poem more striking. This speaker becomes terribly involved in the feud with his ex-friend. Look at the way the **word order** and **syntax** in the line 'In the morning glad I see' throws the emphasis onto 'glad' to suggest the speaker's glee as he views his dead enemy.

Review

Let's review some of the key words and ideas for this poem:

- **rhyme**
- **quatrain**
- **symbol**
- **syntax**
- **extended image**.

Make sure you understand each term clearly. Make a list of definitions which you can use for revision.

'The Five Students' by Thomas Hardy

> **Context**
> Hardy's wife of nearly 40 years, Emma, had just died when he wrote this poem, and he picked up the phrase 'fair She' from something she wrote about herself. It seems he imagined both Emma and himself among the 'Five Students'.

ACTIVITY 5

Understanding the poem

1. As the five students walk through the countryside the seasons change. Identify the season in each verse. How is the changing of the seasons appropriate to what happens in the poem?
2. List the verbs, starting with 'strenuously we stride', which are used for the way the students move on their journey. What do these words tell us about the attitudes they have to their journey?
3. Describe the atmosphere in verse 5. How does Hardy's use of language help to create this atmosphere? (The samples on these pages include possible responses.)
4. How would you explain the poem's title?
5. 'The rest – anon' ends the poem. 'Anon' is an archaic word for 'soon'. What does the final line mean? Could 'rest' possibly have a second meaning?

Moving up the grades

Look again at 'The Five Students' by Thomas Hardy, which deals with the theme of growing old.

For these responses, the key term of the question was **growing old**. This is not the only question that could be asked on this poem. Read the question on your examination paper carefully.

> The atmosphere in verse 5 is very cold and dreary which is suitable to old age. Hardy mentions the icicles on the church roof and the word 'hoarse' suggests the sore throats you get in winter. The third line is very long and slow and there is a rhyming couplet 'gone/anon' to give the poem a definite ending.

This response gained a mark in Band 2. It comments on a few relevant points but does not develop these comments nor explain what the effects are. For example, how is the slowness of the third line achieved? Who is moving slowly and why? What is the significance of 'gone/anon'?

> By the final verse we are in the depths of winter and this season is thought of as similar to the final stage of human life. The setting moves away from the woods and paths of earlier verses towards the church, and perhaps the graveyard. There is ice on the roof and 'on the church-aisle leads' reminds me of the lead coffins used in Hardy's day. 'Gibbers' is an interesting word used for the noise made by the rope on the flag-pole. It means chattering in an idiotic, meaningless way and adds to the cold and depressing atmosphere. The long line that follows has hyphenated words that make it difficult to say. Life does get more difficult as people grow older. The word 'course' is a good choice. A course is something that must be finished, not the pleasant walk of the early verses. And the rhyme with the long vowel 'gone/ anon' ends the poem like a funeral bell which marks the end of life and the end of growing old.

Student is keen to comment on poet's choice of words, and does so well.

*Maintains focus on key term **growing old**.*

This response moved into Band 4 because it focuses on the key term **growing old** and discusses the effects of poetic techniques. (There is also a little contextual material in the reference to lead coffins.) There is a lot of content in this answer, although some of the points could have been developed and expressed a little better.

The image of life as a journey is very common, but what Hardy does in this poem is to combine this image with the image of the seasons matching the stages of human life.

Review

Let's review some of the key words and ideas for this poem:

- **imagery**
- **couplet**
- **setting**.

Make sure you understand each term clearly. Make a list of definitions which you can use for revision.

'La Belle Dame sans Merci' by John Keats

> **Context**
> Keats wrote 'La Belle Dame sans Merci' shortly after the death of his brother Tom from tuberculosis; the 'family disease' as the poet called it. It was a period of dark nightmares, of paleness, fever and sweating for Keats, perhaps the onset of the tuberculosis that he suffered from later in life. In the poem, Love and Death are seen together.
>
> If you search for an image of 'La Belle Dame sans Merci' you will find dozens of images derived from this poem. Why do you think Keats's poem has proved to be so influential with artists over the past 200 years?

ACTIVITY 6

Understanding the poem

1. There are two speakers in the poem. One asks a question, the second answers it with a long explanation. Work out what the question is and where the answer begins.
2. Two meetings, a dream and an awakening – this is the sequence of events in the poem. Make short notes under each of these headings.
3. Keats deliberately chose to use **archaic**, **medieval** words in this poem, although he wrote it in 1819. Find some examples of these and list them. Why do you think Keats chose to use such words?
4. What do the details of the knight's appearance suggest to you? Does the knight's dream back up your impression? Give reasons for your opinions.
5. How is the supernatural quality of the Lady and her power over the knight conveyed? What words convey the danger she represents? (Write your own answer first and then compare it with the sample response opposite.)

Moving up the grades

For these responses the key term of the question was **a sense of the supernatural**. This is not the only question that could be asked on this poem. Read the question on your examination paper carefully.

Poetic technique

This Band 5 response engages with the poet's technique (**rhythm**), gives examples, and develops a discussion of the effects of that short final line to the verse.

> The most interesting thing about the form of the poem is the rhythm and the way the verses end unexpectedly. The first three lines have four beats each, but the fourth has only two or three, so the ending of the verse arrives very suddenly. Sometimes this means that we are left with only a few words to think about, and we realise their importance: 'I love thee true' or 'Hath thee in thrall'. The ending of the last verse is identical to the ending of the first, which gives a nice pattern, but the words 'And no birds sing' leave us with a memory of the eerie, empty landscape where the knight found himself on waking.

This is a sample response to Question 5:

> The Lady is connected with the supernatural early in the poem when the knight twice uses the word 'faery' to describe her. Later the word 'elfin' is used in describing where she lives – 'her elfin grot'. The archaic spelling of 'faery' suggests that she is a creature from long ago. Her French name, too, may suggest that she is a dangerous ('sans merci') and evil enchantress, and so too, perhaps, do her 'wild eyes' and her skill with strange herbs. The knight seems to be guessing that she told him that she loved him, but if she did, her love destroyed him. Her power is suggested by the effect she had on the knight, who is described as 'so haggard and so woe-begone'. While he was with her he was obsessed: 'And nothing else saw all day long'. The Lady's power is most clearly shown in the voices in the knight's dream, and particularly in the ominous words 'in thrall', which means enslaved or enthralled, and perhaps enchanted. If the pale kings in the dream are also her victims, she has great power, judging by their 'starv'd lips' and gaping mouths. They seem to be hungry even in death....

Examiner's tip!
Take care to **develop** the points you make so as to get full value from them.

This response on the Lady **develops** its points (supernatural, power, danger) through apt quotation, discussion and a little analysis of language.

Review

Let's review some of the key words and ideas for this poem:

- **rhythm**
- **medieval**
- **archaic**.

Make sure you understand each term clearly. Make a list of definitions which you can use for revision.

'Bredon Hill' by A.E. Housman

> **Context**
> 'Bredon Hill' is from a collection of poems titled *A Shropshire Lad* published in 1896 but which became very popular during the First World War. The simplicity of the style and the main theme of the nearness of death seemed to appeal to soldiers and their families.

ACTIVITY 7

Understanding the poem

1. This is another poem in which the season changes. Make notes on this change and suggest why Housman builds it into his poem.
2. The church bells ring throughout the poem, but the meaning of the ringing also changes. Show that this is so, referring to the poem to back up what you say.
3. In verse 4 the speaker seems to be trying to make a bargain with the church bells. What is this bargain?
4. What is the event described in verses 5 and 6 and how does the poet convey its significance?
5. 'And I would turn and answer/Among the springing thyme'. Does the phrase 'springing thyme' seem to you to have a second meaning? Explain.
6. What do you think is the tone of the speaker in the final two lines?

Moving up the grades

For this response the key term of the question was **the natural world**. This is not the only question that could be asked on this poem. Read the question on your examination paper carefully.

This sample is from a Band 2 response. It is comparing and contrasting 'Bredon Hill' and 'The Five Students':

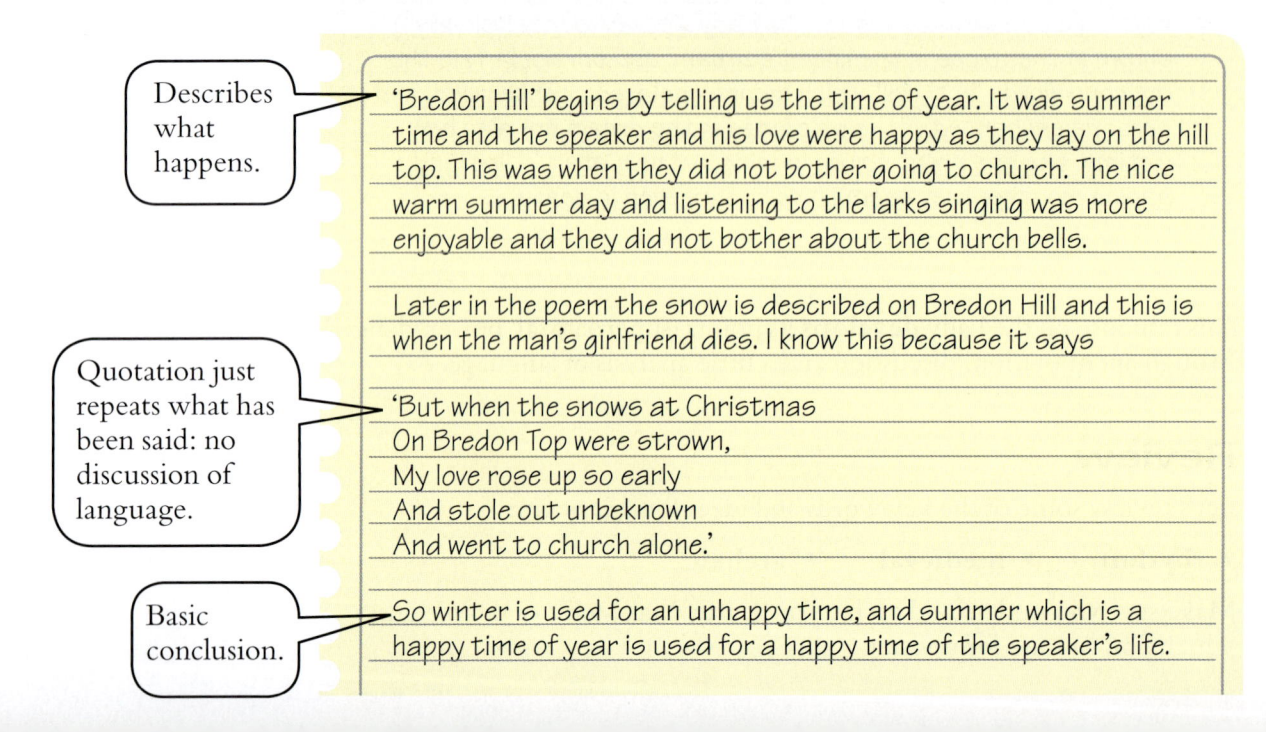

Describes what happens.

'Bredon Hill' begins by telling us the time of year. It was summer time and the speaker and his love were happy as they lay on the hill top. This was when they did not bother going to church. The nice warm summer day and listening to the larks singing was more enjoyable and they did not bother about the church bells.

Later in the poem the snow is described on Bredon Hill and this is when the man's girlfriend dies. I know this because it says

Quotation just repeats what has been said: no discussion of language.

'But when the snows at Christmas
On Bredon Top were strown,
My love rose up so early
And stole out unbeknown
And went to church alone.'

Basic conclusion.

So winter is used for an unhappy time, and summer which is a happy time of year is used for a happy time of the speaker's life.

> This is like 'The Five Students' by Thomas Hardy. I mean the way the seasons change. At the start of Hardy's poem the sun is shining 'passionate-eyed' and everyone is happy. But later when everyone is old or dead, it is winter 'icicles'.

Quotation not integrated into sentence.

This is a basic response. It describes and paraphrases, and discusses the background of the seasons in a simple way. It shows awareness of language, but this does not go beyond quotation. It makes a simple connection between the poems but needs to develop this and show in more detail how the poems are similar and how they differ – for example, Hardy's greater use of seasonal imagery and Housman's use of the church bell as a reminder in all seasons.

Review

Let's review some of the key words and ideas for this poem:

- **personification**
- **ambiguous**
- **natural imagery**.

Make sure you understand each term clearly. Make a list of definitions which you can use for revision.

'The Cap and Bells' by W.B. Yeats

Context

This poem comes from Yeats's attempt to remember one of his dreams. He was interested in dreams, visions and mysticism all his life, and believed that wisdom could be found there. The wisdom in this poem seems to be that if we try to impress in love, we fail in love. Love makes a fool of us and we must admit that. This message is found many times in Yeats's poems.

The cap and bells is the traditional uniform worn by the jester or fool of past centuries. This poem seems to have a setting inspired by medieval illustrations. The medieval artists loved painting gardens and towers, and were fond of bright reds and blues.

Like many symbolic poems this one is mysterious, and the meaning, like the meaning of dreams, is waiting to be revealed.

ACTIVITY 8

Understanding the poem

1. The jester sends three gifts to the young queen. What are they and what is her reaction to each of them?
2. What contrasts do you notice in the descriptions of the first two gifts? Can you suggest why so much is different?
3. What do you think the owl **symbolises**?
4. Is the garden an appropriate setting? Give reasons for your opinion.
5. In the **image** of the heart 'in a red and quivering garment', what does the word 'quivering' suggest to you?
6. With what attitude does the jester send his final gift?
7. What does the **image** of stars 'growing out of the air' convey to you?
8. How do you interpret the last two verses of the poem?

Moving up the grades

This sample is comparing and contrasting 'The Cap and Bells' with 'La Belle Dame sans Merci'. The key term of the question is **love for another person**. This is not the only question that could be asked on these poems. Read the question on your examination paper carefully.

> The jester courts the queen by giving her gifts – these are how he expresses his love for her. The gifts are his soul and his heart. We still say to love with heart and soul, meaning to love totally and unconditionally. Yeats, by using the word 'wise-tongued' to describe the soul, and 'sweet-tongued' to describe the heart shows how valuable the gifts were.
>
> The knight in 'La Belle Dame' also gives gifts to his lady. They are not great gifts, as in 'The Cap and Bells', but he made her

Begins to develop contrast.

> 'a garland for her head/And bracelets too and fragrant zone'. These seem to be flowers, a traditional gift between lovers and he receives gifts back 'honey wild and manna dew'. The important difference is the result that love for another person has on the lover.
>
> The jester, when he sends his last present to the queen expects to die, but the happy ending when the queen is described as in love shows that he won't. Whereas the knight in 'La Belle Dame' is left unhappy and perhaps dying. Keats's metaphor of the fading rose shows this.

Maintains focus on question.

Comments briefly on language.

This is part of a Band 3 response. It carries out the comparison and contrast with determination and develops the argument. There is certainly some focus on the question. To improve further, there should be more analysis of language, for example the imagery in the ending of 'The Cap and Bells'.

Examiner's tip!

Bring the writer's name into your discussion.

Review

Let's review some of the key words and ideas for this poem:

- **symbol**
- **setting**
- **metaphor**.

Make sure you understand each term clearly. Make a list of definitions which you can use for revision.

'Out, Out' by Robert Frost

> **Context**
> Robert Frost lived on a farm in New England in the early years of the twentieth century and the way of life described in the poem was well known to him. At this time, children were expected to help with the farm work – 'doing a man's work'.
> The title refers to Macbeth's despairing speech at the end of that play where he believes that life is meaningless.

ACTIVITY 9

Understanding the poem

1 The boy is described as a 'big boy/ Doing a man's work, though a child at heart'. At what moments in the poem do you get a sense that the boy is a 'child at heart'? Refer to the words of the poem.

2 What was the boy 'old enough to know'?

3 Using this saw obviously has its dangers. Are there any hints in the poem that the concentration of the workers may be slackening? (The sample below includes a possible response.)

4 Show how the saw is **personified** in the poem. Refer to the words and phrases used. What impression of the saw does this give?

5 What is the effect of the exclamation 'But the hand!' in the description of the accident?

6 What do you think of the reactions of the farm people to the boy's death? Pick out any words or phrases that seem striking to you.

Moving up the grades

Look again at 'Out Out' by Robert Frost which deals with **attitudes to death**.

> The danger of using the saw is hinted at in the menacing verbs used to describe its running ('snarled and rattled'). Obviously, operating it needs one hundred per cent concentration. Frost suggests distractions in the 'sweet scent' of the cut wood, and more clearly in the lines about lifting eyes. Lifting eyes would be a most dangerous thing to do when operating a buzz-saw. Later in the poem, the speaker suggests that the boy was longing to be let off the last half-hour, and that time 'saved from work' is something that a boy values a great deal. Finally, the moment of the accident is when the sister says 'Supper.' She comes into the poem suddenly, and her word may have been unexpected and had something to do with the accident.

This Band 4 response sustains its focus on the question of 'slackening concentration' all the way through. It backs up its points with apt reference at times. The student has been a careful reader and makes reasonable inferences about what happened in the farmyard. The final point is an interesting one, but it is vaguely expressed ('something to do with') and needs fuller explanation.

Sentence length

At the beginning of this poem, Frost is **describing**. It was the end of the day and 'nothing happened'. The atmosphere in the yard was perhaps tired or a little lazy and the sentences match this atmosphere: they are long, trailing over several lines and picking up pleasant details of how the cut wood smelt and the view of the mountains under the sunset sky. Until the accident, the saw is just a noise in the background.

You can contrast these long descriptive sentences with what we find at the end of the poem, where almost every sentence is a short, flat statement, perhaps to express the numbness and shock felt by the rest of the family. Only the final sentence is more than a simple statement. Look at this sentence, especially at the 'extra' part of it: 'since they were not the one dead'. What might the speaker be implying?

Review

Let's review some of the key words and ideas for this poem:

- **onomatopoeia**
- **blank verse**
- **anticlimax**
- **personification**.

Make sure you understand each term clearly. Make a list of definitions which you can use for revision.

'Piazza Piece' by John Crowe Ransom

> **Context**
> The setting of this **sonnet** – the moonlit piazza with roses or vines on the window-trellis – seems to locate us in the past, in the formal courtship rituals of Italy, with the lover speaking up to his lady at her window (as in the famous balcony scene in *Romeo and Juliet*). Ransom has chosen a suitable form for his poem, for it was in Italy that the sonnet developed, and it was often used for the theme of love.

ACTIVITY 10

Understanding the poem

1. Why are the characters referred to as 'gentleman and lady', rather than 'boy and girl' or 'man and woman'?
2. What words and phrases convey the sinister quality of the gentleman? How are his words about the roses and the moon significant?
3. Why do you think the lady finds the gentleman's words 'dry and faint as in a dream'?
4. What threat does the lady make, and how effective will that threat be?
5. What does the repetition of the first and last lines of both the **octave** and the **sestet** suggest to you?

Moving up the grades

For this response, the key term of the question was **death** and the student interpreted the old man in the poem as a **personification** of death. This is not the only question that could be asked on this poem. Read the question on your examination paper carefully.

This is part of a Band 3 response:

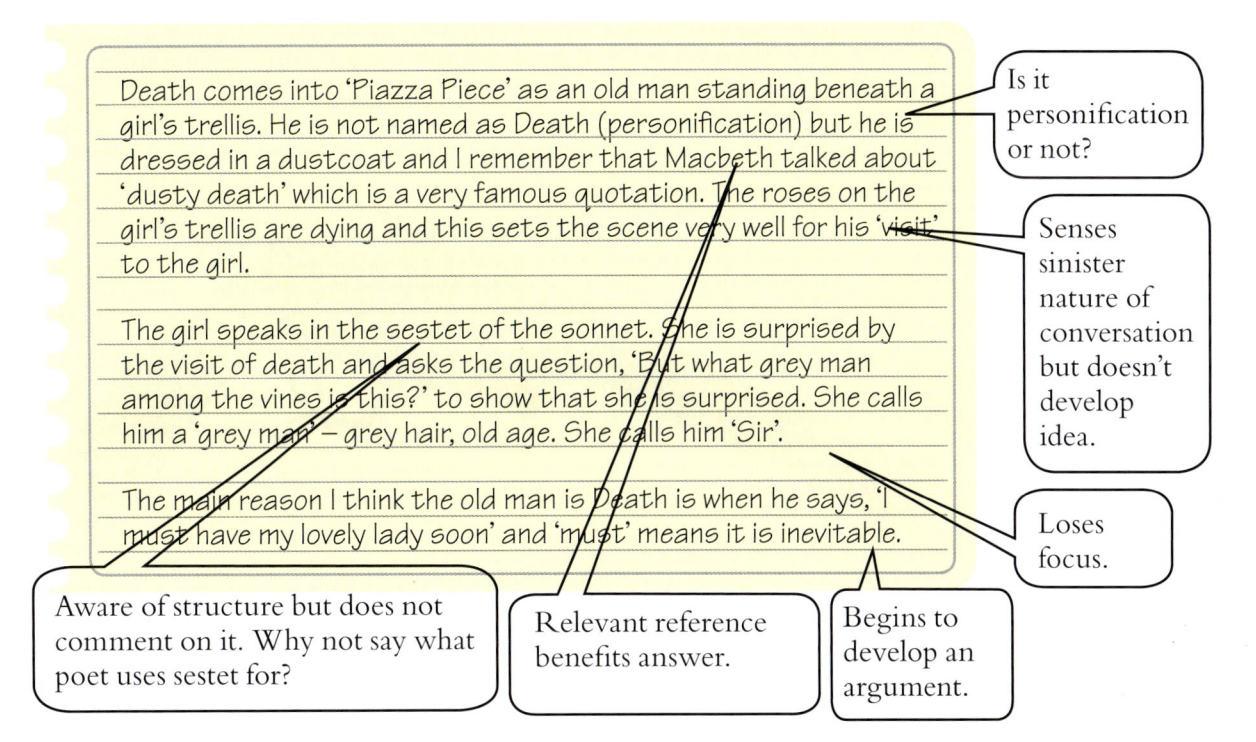

> Death comes into 'Piazza Piece' as an old man standing beneath a girl's trellis. He is not named as Death (personification) but he is dressed in a dustcoat and I remember that Macbeth talked about 'dusty death' which is a very famous quotation. The roses on the girl's trellis are dying and this sets the scene very well for his 'visit' to the girl.
>
> The girl speaks in the sestet of the sonnet. She is surprised by the visit of death and asks the question, 'But what grey man among the vines is this?' to show that she is surprised. She calls him a 'grey man' – grey hair, old age. She calls him 'Sir'.
>
> The main reason I think the old man is Death is when he says, 'I must have my lovely lady soon' and 'must' means it is inevitable.

Annotations:
- Is it personification or not?
- Senses sinister nature of conversation but doesn't develop idea.
- Loses focus.
- Aware of structure but does not comment on it. Why not say what poet uses sestet for?
- Relevant reference benefits answer.
- Begins to develop an argument.

This response just made it into Band 3 and the student may have been disappointed because there are certainly good things in it. For example the final paragraph begins to say something which would be powerfully relevant to the question, but then just stops. And the references to poetic technique and the structure of the poem could have earned much more credit if the student had explained how the poet *uses* them in presenting death.

Examiner's tip!

Bring the name of the poet into it. This can help remind you of what you ought to be doing when you are writing about technique.

Review

Let's review some of the key words and ideas for this poem:

- repetition
- sound effects
- sonnet
- octave
- sestet
- personification.

Make sure you understand each term clearly. Make a list of definitions which you can use for revision.

'Richard Cory' by Edwin Arlington Robinson

> **Context**
> This is one of Robinson's poems about individual inhabitants of the fictional small town of Tilbury and their hidden tragedies. These poems are sometimes cryptic and puzzling, leaving us wondering about the suffering that goes on beneath the surface of everyday life. Robinson's aim, he suggests in another poem, is to tell us more about a human being by saying less.

ACTIVITY 11
Understanding the poem

1 Who in your opinion is the speaker in the poem?

2 Write a paragraph on Richard Cory under the following headings – appearance, wealth, his manner towards others, the effect he had on others.

3 Discuss the poet's choice of words in the phrases 'imperially slim' and 'he glittered when he walked'.

4 Why might these lines be ironic: 'he was everything/ To make us wish that we were in his place'?

5 What do lines 13–14 tell us about the situation of the speaker and of people like him? How do these lines add to the shock of the two lines which follow?

Moving up the grades

This is part of a Band 3 response to a question with the key term **the unexpectedness of death**. This is not the only question that could be asked on this poem. Read the question on your examination paper carefully.

This student chose to compare and contrast 'Out, Out' with 'Richard Cory'.

> In the description of the work on the farm in Frost's poem the saw is certainly menacing and the choice of the onomatopoeic words 'snarl' and 'rattle' create the impression that it is both a machine and an animal. When it attacks the boy, Frost uses personification and says it 'leapt', and this sudden movement increases the unexpectedness of the accident that causes the boy's death.
>
> 'Richard Cory' on the other hand, had everything. He was a wealthy man in the town and Robinson uses memorable phrases to express how glamorous he was, such as 'imperially slim'. He seems to be wearing diamonds as he 'glittered when he walked'. The poem ends with the completely unexpected death of Richard Cory:
>
> 'And Richard Cory one calm summer night
> Went home and put a bullet through his head.'
>
> When Robinson tells us that this violent death happened on a 'calm summer night' he is increasing the unexpectedness of the death because of the contrast.

Annotations:
- Good discussion of language, but needs to focus from start on key term.
- Better focus here.
- Looks as if student is making a contrast – but nothing is actually contrasted!
- Using the poet's name helps here in making a relevant point about poetic technique.

The problem with this response is that it does not really compare and contrast the poems (though it pretends to at the beginning of the second paragraph). The argument is undeveloped: the student says that the death of the boy was an unexpected accident, but does not make the contrasting point that the death of Richard Cory, while it was unexpected by the townspeople, was not an accident. So, although there is good work done on use of language, it is likely that this response will stay in Band 3.

Additional Context
There is a recording of 'Richard Cory' by Paul Simon which expands the character of the speaker. You may wish to search it out, but remember, your concern is with the poem.

Review

Let's review some of the key words and ideas for this poem:

- **alternate rhyme**
- **contrast**
- **simple connectives** – 'and', 'but', 'so'.

Make sure you understand each term clearly. Make a list of definitions which you can use for revision.

'Night of the Scorpion' by Nissim Ezekiel

> **Context**
> The sack of rice, the scorpion and the mud-baked walls suggest a **setting** for the poem. Nissim Ezekiel grew up in Bombay. The communal life of an Indian village is suggested by its reaction to this family emergency. The mother's love emerges triumphantly at the end of the poem – but only after the noise dies down!

ACTIVITY 12

Understanding the poem

1. The stinging of the speaker's mother happens so quickly that it is not even described. How does the poet convey the suddenness of the event?
2. What does the **simile** 'like swarms of flies' suggest to you about the villagers? How is the comparison continued later in the sentence?
3. What does the repetition of 'they said' suggest to you about the behaviour of the villagers?
4. The villagers are described as having 'the peace of understanding on each face'. What do you think might be the **tone** of the speaker at this point?
5. Write a description of what the father does. In what way is it surprising?
6. Many different cures are attempted. List them. What do you think the speaker believes to be the reason for his mother's survival?

Moving up the grades

This is the end of a Band 3 response. The key term of the question was **love**. This is not the only question that could be asked on this poem. Read the question on your examination paper carefully.

This student chose to compare and contrast 'Night of the Scorpion' with 'Bredon Hill'.

> … The kinds of love are different in these two poems. In 'Night of the Scorpion' it is the love of a mother for her children. The speaker is one of these children and we see the events through his or her eyes. Most of the poem is about the noisy neighbours who come along, thinking that they can help. Although the mother is described as being 'in the centre', she seems to be forgotten about in a way and it is only at the very end of the poem that she speaks, when she thanks God that the scorpion spared her children. This is very generous, unconditional love like we expect a mother's love to be.
>
> 'Bredon Hill' is set in the English countryside, a great contrast to the Indian village in 'Night of the Scorpion'. It is a much quieter poem. There is only the sound of the church bells and the singing birds, which is another contrast because in Nissim Ezekiel's poem there was a lot of noise from the neighbours, as I have said. The kind of love described is also different. It is a man's love for a woman not a mother for a child. The ending is unhappy as the woman dies. The ending of 'Night of the Scorpion' is not unhappy at all, though the mother has to go through a lot of pain.
>
> The poem which affected me more has to be 'Night of the Scorpion' because there is no selfishness in the mother's love. I really enjoyed the ending of the poem when the mother speaks. I am not saying that the love in 'Bredon Hill' is selfish, but the lovers are in their own little bubble so it might be.

Focuses on key term and says a little about poetic technique.

Develops comparisons and contrasts.

Expresses preference and explains it, but could develop explanation.

This response works successfully at comparing and contrasting the poems, and ends with an interesting personal response. With more attention to use of language it could move up into Band 4.

Examiner's tip!
Don't forget to give reasons for your preference.

Review

Let's review some of the key words and ideas for this poem:

- **setting**
- **metaphor**
- **simile**
- **alliteration**
- **onomatopoeia**.

Make sure you understand each term clearly. Make a list of definitions which you can use for revision.

'Those Winter Sundays' by Robert E. Hayden

Context
The African-American poet Robert Hayden was brought up in a slum area of Detroit by foster-parents, in a household that was often violent and unhappy. This poem, however, deals with a man's regret at his own lack of understanding when he was a child.

ACTIVITY 13

Understanding the poem

1 What was unpleasant about the experience of the speaker's father in the first verse? What does the word 'too' tell us?

2 What do the words 'splintering, breaking' suggest about the morning cold in the house?

3 What phrase best conveys the fact that family life in this household was not happy?

4 Which words and phrases suggest the attitude of family members towards the father?

5 What does the repeated question at the end of the poem suggest about the attitude of the speaker to his father's actions?

6 The word 'love' is used in the last line of the poem. What have you learnt about love from this poem?

Moving up the grades

This is part of a Band 4 response to a question with the key term **unhappy love**. This is not the only question that could be asked on this poem. Read the question on your examination paper carefully.

> Sustains focus on key term throughout.

The love is from the father and we get the impression that it was unhappy from the ungrateful way he was treated. 'No-one ever thanked him' gets a sentence of its own to emphasise it and is placed at the end of a verse for the same reason. The physical conditions reinforce the impression of unhappiness, and words like 'blueblack', 'cold splintering' and 'cracked hands' show the discomfort. But the most hard-hitting line for the unhappiness of this love is the one about the boy 'fearing the chronic angers of that house'. Hayden describes the boy speaking 'indifferently' to his father just after he had got up in the cold and polished his son's shoes out of love. The poem ends by describing the father's love as 'austere and lonely offices'. 'Offices' here means things that are done for other people. These are things that this father does out of love for his son — but in this case they are not happy. It is sad that there is no sign that the boy loved his father. Hayden ends the poem with a question 'What did I know?' and this suggests to me that the boy feels sorry that he never even thanked his father.

> Comments on effects of poetic techniques.

> Identifies important line but does not analyse it.

> Evidence of close study: unusual words have been looked up.

The argument is developed and focused on the question and there is enough discussion of the effects of the poet's use of language to confirm this in Band 4.

Review

Let's review some of the key words and ideas for this poem:

- **use of speaker**
- **varied sentence length**
- **rhetorical question**.

Make sure you understand each term clearly. Make a list of definitions which you can use for revision.

'Love Song: I and Thou' by Alan Dugan

> **Context**
> The title of this poem has an obvious meaning, but Dugan may be reminding us of the philosopher Martin Buber's work *I and Thou*, in which he says that life finds its meaning in relationships. Or Dugan may even be reminding us of the *Rubaiyat of Omar Khayyam*, where the presence of the poet's lover helps him turn an unhappy wilderness into paradise.
> Dugan's poetry is often marked by plain and direct language.

ACTIVITY 14

Understanding the poem

1. This poem describes the speaker's feelings about the building of a house. At the end of the poem he confesses that there are things he cannot do, and admits what he needs. What, in your view, is the **metaphorical** meaning of this house?
2. What does the **simile** describing the bent nails suggest about the speaker's state of mind? How is this suggestion continued by the beginning of the next sentence?
3. Explain the phrase: 'I danced with a purple thumb'.
4. Is there a second meaning to the last two lines? Think of the ways we use the phrase 'to nail something'.
5. How would you describe the change of tone at the end of the poem? Refer to particular words and phrases from the poem.

Moving up the grades

For this response, the key term of the question was **poems about love that surprised you**. This is not the only question that could be asked on this poem. Read the question on your examination paper carefully.

This is part of a low Band 3 response:

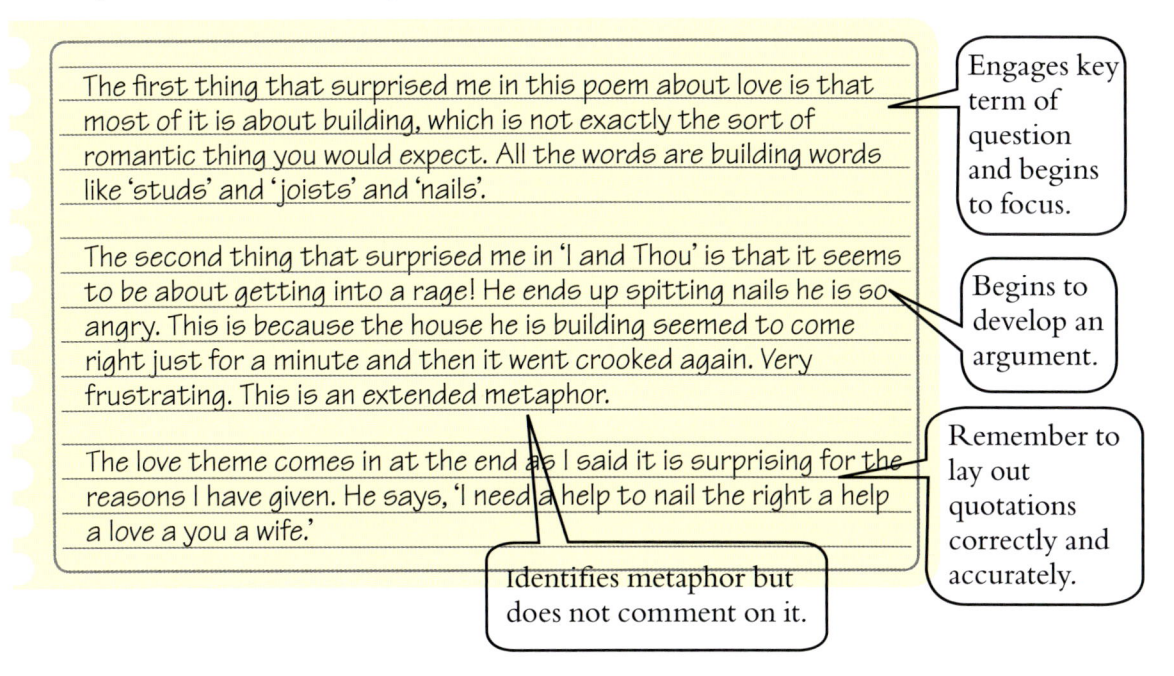

> The first thing that surprised me in this poem about love is that most of it is about building, which is not exactly the sort of romantic thing you would expect. All the words are building words like 'studs' and 'joists' and 'nails'.
>
> The second thing that surprised me in 'I and Thou' is that it seems to be about getting into a rage! He ends up spitting nails he is so angry. This is because the house he is building seemed to come right just for a minute and then it went crooked again. Very frustrating. This is an extended metaphor.
>
> The love theme comes in at the end as I said it is surprising for the reasons I have given. He says, 'I need a help to nail the right a help a love a you a wife.'

Engages key term of question and begins to focus.

Begins to develop an argument.

Identifies metaphor but does not comment on it.

Remember to lay out quotations correctly and accurately.

This student is only just beginning to comment on use of language. There is a lot of work to do here. Fortunately the response has other stronger points. The student knows to focus on the question, and is beginning to build an argument.

Review

Let's review some of the key words and ideas for this poem:

- **simile**
- **repetition**
- **extended metaphor**
- **use of technical terms** – from house building
- **religious references**
- **use of paradox** – 'I/Will live in it until it kills me.'

Make sure you understand each term clearly. Make a list of definitions which you can use for revision.

Unit 2 Section B: Poetry

Assessment Matrix – Higher Tier Unit 2 – Section B: Poetry

Assessment Objective	Band 0 Mark [0]	Band 1: Very Little [1]–[10]	Band 2: Emerging [11]–[18]	Band 3: Competent [19]–[26]	Band 4: Good [27]–[34]	Band 5: Excellent [35]–[40]
AO1 Argument	Response not worthy of credit	Some writing about text or task Very basic level of accuracy in written expression and coherence of response. Form mostly appropriate	Attempt to focus on content Simple, straightforward, or limited response Assertion, basic conclusion, narrative or description, quotation and/or paraphrase Fairly sound level of accuracy in written expression and coherence of response. Form mostly appropriate	Begins to focus on relevant content Begins to develop a response Some argument Competent level of accuracy in written expression and coherence of response. Form mostly appropriate	Sustained focus on relevant content Reasoned response Developed argument An appropriate form of response which is clearly constructed and accurately expressed	Persuasive, coherent answer to the question set Evaluative response Sustained argument An appropriate form of response which is clearly constructed and expressed with fluency and precision

Anthology 1: Love and Death

AO2 **Form and Language**	Response not worthy of credit	Simplistic remarks about content Little or no awareness of structure, form or poetic techniques	Some awareness of content Some awareness of structure, form or poetic techniques Occasional reference to poet's words	Comments on content Explains structure, form or poetic technique Some understanding of the poet's use of language	Interpretation of content Comments on the effects of structure, form or poetic techniques Comments on language and style, with the emergence of a critical vocabulary	Assured interpretation of content Discussion on the effects of structure, form or poetic techniques Analysis of the poet's language and style, using appropriate critical terminology
AO3 **Comparison and Contrast**	Response not worthy of credit	Poems considered in isolation	Simple connections made between poems	Makes obvious comparisons and contrasts between poems	Responds to opportunities to compare and contrast poems	A synthesised approach to detailed comparison and contrast
AO4 **Awareness of Context**	Response not worthy of credit	No contextual material	Contextual material is present though not incorporated in argument	Some attempt to incorporate contextual material in argument	Selective use of contextual material to enhance argument	Response is enriched by use of contextual material

Anthology 2: Nature and War

'The Attack' by Siegfried Sassoon

Context
Infantry (foot-soldier) attacks in the First World War were preceded by artillery barrages, intended to demoralise the enemy and drive them underground. Sassoon served as an infantry officer on the Western Front. In his war poetry he tried to tell the truth about the terrifying experience of war.

ACTIVITY 15

Understanding the poem

1. How is an ominous atmosphere created in the first three and a half lines? Refer to the poet's word choice and use of **personification**.
2. What do the verbs 'creep and topple' suggest about the movement of the tanks?
3. In lines 6–8, how does the poet convey how difficult it was for the soldiers to move?
4. The enemy fire is described as 'bristling'. What does this word suggest?
5. There is obvious use of **alliteration** in line 11. What does the line mean and what is the effect of the alliteration?
6. Write about the last two lines of the poem, showing how the poet uses language to bring out the horror of the experience for the soldiers.
7. Why do you think Sassoon uses the **present tense** in this poem?

Moving up the grades

For these responses, the key term of the question was **attitudes to war**. This is not the only question that could be asked on this poem. Read the question on your examination paper carefully.

This is an extract from a Band 2 response:

> The poem is about an attack during a battle in the First World War when Sassoon was a soldier and he is describing what he saw happening around him in the trenches. He describes the tanks and the sound of the guns 'the barrage roars and lifts' and then describes the soldiers. We can imagine these frightened soldiers with their heavy packs and this image is the opposite of what people at home believed because they thought of their soldiers as proud heroes not like these soldiers.

*Describes content but does not focus on **attitudes to war**.*

Some relevant reference to contextual information.

This response has some relevant information which could support an argument, but does not address the key term of the question – **attitudes to war**. There is some reference to the poet's language and the beginnings of a good point about the sounds created in the poem, but these points are not developed.

A Band 4 response will discuss points in depth, for example:

> Sassoon's attitude to war is clearly presented in his description of the soldiers in this poem. They are described in pitiable terms 'clumsily bowed', 'Lines of grey, muttering faces, masked with fear'. These aren't the heroes of the newspapers back home, but the 'cannon fodder' who died in their thousands on the battlefields of the Somme and Thiepval. Sassoon wanted to let people see what these poor soldiers really had to go through. The use of alliteration and the repetition of 'and' in line 7 emphasises the weight of their kit and adds to the atmosphere of oppressive fear which highlights Sassoon's attitude that war is not glorious, but terrifying and brutal. The final half-line of the poem brings home Sassoon's attitude to war with the sudden personal exclamation 'O Jesus, make it stop!' which forces us to see the desperation of the individual soldiers.

Sustains focus on key term of question.

Uses contextual information to enhance argument.

Comments on effects of poetic technique.

This student sustains focus on the question and ensures that the examiner sees this by repeating the key term. The student also brings the poet's name into the discussion, thus remaining focused on technique and use of language. It is interesting to note how the contextual information has been carefully selected and integrated into a discussion of Sassoon's 'attitude to war'. To improve this answer, the student could develop the discussion of the emotive appeal of the end of the poem.

Examiner's tip!

Remember to express **your** personal response to the poem.

Review

Let's review some of the key words and ideas for this poem:

- **personification**
- **alliteration**
- **present tense**.

Make sure you understand each term clearly. Make a list of definitions which you can use for revision.

'An Irish Airman Foresees His Death' by W.B. Yeats

> **Context**
> This poem was written in memory of Robert Gregory, son of Yeats's friend Lady Gregory, who was killed in action in 1918. Note that the poem says very little about the war itself. It may reflect the complex feelings of some Irishmen towards the conflict they were engaged in. It was published in 1919.

ACTIVITY 16

Understanding the poem

1. What reason does the speaker give for his lack of strong feelings about the war?
2. What reason does he give for fighting, and how does this reason differ from the more common reasons listed in the poem?
3. Flying early aircraft without modern instruments depended much on balance. 'I balanced all' is a key phrase towards the end of the poem. Show how the speaker balances opposites in his mind (positive points and negative points) in deciding to fly, and fight, and die. Show how the poet's use of rhyme plays its part in this balancing of opposites. What other examples of balance can you find in the poem?
4. The poem is written in **iambic tetrameter**. What effect does this create for the reader?
5. How would you sum up the speaker's attitude towards his death?

Moving up the grades

This is part of a Band 4 response to a question where the key term was **attitudes to war**. This is not the only question that could be asked on this poem. Read the question on your examination paper carefully.

> [Sustains focus on speaker's **attitude to war**.]
>
> The speaker's attitude to war is almost indifferent. We can see that he has not joined the fighting for the usual reasons, for example because of patriotism 'Those that I guard I do not love' or a sense of duty 'Nor law, nor duty bade me fight'. It is almost as if the speaker feels that the war itself is not important. His attitude seems to be more personal 'A lonely impulse of delight/ Drove to this tumult in the clouds'. At this time, aeroplanes were new to the theatre of war and pilots were aware that their chances of survival were slim. This knowledge is evident in the attitude of the airman in the poem, as he seems to find 'delight' in the thrill of flying and has no fear of death:
>
> 'I know that I shall meet my fate
> Somewhere among the clouds above'
>
> The poet presents the pilot's almost emotionless consideration of his choice to fight in the war through the steady iambic tetrameter rhythm, which sounds clipped, and the alternating rhyme of the poem. I think it is interesting that the poet has rhymed words which have opposing themes 'fight/delight, crowds/ clouds, breath/death' which emphasises the pilot's careful contemplation of his decision. This is taken further in the final lines where the inverted syntax shows how the speaker has thought carefully about his reasons for fighting. 'I balanced all.../ The years to come seemed waste of breath,/ A waste of breath the years behind/ In balance...'

Annotations:
- Some interpretation of content.
- Relevant contextual information.
- Comments on effects of poetic technique.

This student sustains focus on the key term of the question and explores how the poet presents the speaker's attitude to war. There is some consideration of poetic technique with discussion of the effects of rhyme and rhythm. Comments are supported by carefully selected evidence from the text.

Review

Let's review some of the key words and ideas for this poem:
- use of speaker
- iambic tetrameter
- tone.

Make sure you understand each term clearly. Make a list of definitions which you can use for revision.

'The Field of Waterloo' by Thomas Hardy

> **Context**
> This is an excerpt from an enormous dramatic poem called *The Dynasts*. It describes the battlefield of Waterloo from an unusual perspective. You will notice Hardy's fondness for unusual words several times in this poem, and also his sympathy with small, shy creatures.

ACTIVITY 17

Understanding the poem

1 This poem deals mainly with animals and insects and plants. List the evidence for human activity with a brief note on each piece you find. For example:

> *'the thud of hoofs'* – Although this sounds like animals, it is likely to be warhorses of some kind. Cavalry? Gun-horses? Onomatopoeic use of 'thud' magnifies the impact of their hoofs.

2 Most of the animals mentioned are timid and harmless. What point is the poet making?

3 The **alliteration** of 'foul red flood' alerts the reader's ear to the fact that this is an important moment in the poem. What are we learning at this moment?

4 How would you explain the meaning of 'the day's long rheum'?

5 Life and death seem to mix in the final verse. Pick out the words and phrases that show this. Does the poet's use of rhyme help?

Moving up the grades

For these responses, the key term of the question was **impact of war**. This is not the only question that could be asked on this poem. Read the question on your examination paper carefully.

This is part of a Band 2 response:

> In this poem, it describes the animals and insects which live on the battlefield like the coneys and moles. It shows how they are frightened by the battle and instead of talking about the soldiers fighting, the poem describes the impact the war has on nature. The poet uses words like 'crushed' and 'bruised' to show how the animals have been affected by the battle.

Describes what happens.

Attempts to address key term of question.

This is a simple, straightforward response which shows some awareness of meaning and the words the poet uses, but presents only basic points which are undeveloped. A Band 2 student relies on description, but to improve must go further and comment on meaning and the techniques the poet uses.

Let's consider a Band 4 response:

> Hardy presents a different view of the battlefield by describing the devastating impact the war has on nature. Hardy repeats frightening verbs such as 'crushed' and uses words like 'trodden and bruised' to show that nature is not simply disturbed by the battle but destroyed. He uses the alliterative metaphor 'foul red flood' to describe the blood which soaked the battlefield from the bodies of soldiers but focuses on the 'worm' which is personified – thinking 'him safe'. At first glance, this could be a comical image, but I think the shocking impact of the battle is shown by the use of 'scene so grim' along with the description of the blood – there is so much that it becomes a 'flood' drowning nature.

Sustains focus on key term.

Comments on effect of poetic technique.

Interprets content.

This student is clearly focusing on the key term of the question and discusses the effects of poetic techniques. Notice that quotations are carefully selected and integrated into the response – there is no need to quote large chunks of the poem when a few words or phrases will support the point you are making.

Review

Let's review some of the key words and ideas for this poem:

- **alliteration**
- **metaphor**
- **triplet**
- **perspective**.

Make sure you understand each term clearly. Make a list of definitions which you can use for revision.

'Auguries of Innocence' (extract) by William Blake

Context
One of the beliefs of the visionary poet William Blake was that great truths are to be found in small things – 'a world in a grain of sand'. Blake's hatred of injustice and cruelty can be seen in this extract from a longer poem. Blake was writing at a time when there was very public mistreatment of animals – hare hunting, cockfighting and horses misused on the road are all mentioned. But notice too what Blake says about the effects of cruelty.

ACTIVITY 18

Understanding the poem

1 After the examples of cruelty to animals, the **couplet** 'Every Wolf's & Lion's howl/ Raises from Hell a Human Soul' seems puzzling at first. What do you think Blake means by it?

2 Why does the poet claim that the Lamb 'forgives the Butcher's Knife'?

3 The lines about the bats and owls take us into a new area of the poem. What ideas are being explored in these lines?

4 What is the poet saying about cruelty in the four lines starting 'He who shall hurt the little Wren . . .'?

5 Spiders and flies are acknowledged enemies. Why does Blake seem to suggest an alliance between them?

6 What is your response to the couplet that ends the extract: 'Kill not the Moth nor Butterfly,/ For the Last Judgement draweth nigh.'

7 The repeated couplets seem at first to be just that – repetitive. Does Blake succeed in developing an argument about cruelty? Give your reasons.

8 Why do you think Blake titled the poem 'Auguries of Innocence'?

Moving up the grades

This is an extract from a high Band 4 response to a question which asks students to discuss the idea of **consequences of cruelty**. This is not the only question that could be asked on this topic. Read the question on your examination paper carefully.

> Throughout the poem, the speaker shows how disgusting he feels cruelty to innocent creatures is by describing the consequences of such actions. For example, he hates the idea of wild animals being kept captive: 'A robin redbreast in a cage/ Puts all heaven in a rage.'
>
> It is interesting to note that the consequences aren't 'real' – what evidence is there that heaven would be in 'a rage'? The consequences are spiritual or moral – 'A skylark wounded in the wing,/ A cherubim does cease to sing.' He shows that heaven and God are hurt by mistreatment of nature and God's creatures. The problem is – what if you don't believe in God? If you don't believe in heaven, then you aren't going to worry about the mistreatment of these animals – these consequences have no meaning for an unbeliever. I think part of what Blake is trying to do here is to make people think about the mistreatment of innocent creatures and see such actions as offensive and harmful. Blake wants us to appreciate the beauty of nature and be offended by its mistreatment. But he is also commenting on faith and innocence.

This student sustains focus on the idea of **consequences** and tries to interpret meaning in the poem. There is some argument and discussion of the poet's use of language. The student has carefully selected quotations to support ideas – this is an important skill to develop. Concise, carefully selected quotations are more effective than copying out large sections of the poem in the hope that some of it will back up the point you are making! The final paragraph of the sample response could be developed further.

Review

Let's review some of the key words and ideas for this poem:

- **couplet**
- **paradox**
- **symbol**.

Make sure you understand each term clearly. Make a list of definitions which you can use for revision.

'Composed Upon Westminster Bridge' by William Wordsworth

Context
This **sonnet** is dated 3 September 1802. It was written at a time when people believed that beautiful scenery was to be looked for in rugged, lonely and remote areas. Wordsworth was reversing this attitude to beauty by finding it in a great city – though you might notice that he seems to have left out the people who lived there.

ACTIVITY 19

Understanding the poem

1. In structure, sonnets are often divided into an **octave** (lines 1–8) and a **sestet** (lines 9–14), with the two sections dealing with different aspects of the subject. Discuss whether that is the case here.
2. Look at the **simile** in line 4. What things are being compared? What does the simile imply about the city?
3. How does the poet try to make the boundaries between the city and the countryside disappear? Refer to the words of the poem.
4. What evidence can you find in the poem that the speaker was looking at London at dawn?
5. What uses of **personification** can you find in the poem? What do they add to it?
6. How does Wordsworth transmit a sense of peace and tranquility to the reader? You could consider the use of long vowel sounds, for example 'glideth'.
7. What is the effect of the use of the exclamation in line 13?
8. When would the sun have been shining in its 'first splendour'? What is the sunshine on that September morning in 1802 being compared to?
9. The poet uses **enjambment** and **caesura** in the octet. What is the effect of these techniques? (The samples on these pages include possible responses.)

Moving up the grades

For these responses, the key term of the question was **reactions to nature**. This is not the only question that could be asked on this poem. Read the question on your examination paper carefully.

> The poet uses enjambment in the poem which means that the meaning carries on to the next line of the poem. For example:
>
> 'Ships, towers, domes, theatres and temples lie
> Open unto the fields,'
>
> The poet also uses a technique called caesura which means that there is a pause in a line of the poem rather than at the end of the line, for example.

> 'This City now doth like a garment wear
> The beauty of the morning: silent, bare,'

This comes from a Band 2 answer. The student is aware of poetic techniques and can identify them in the poem, but to move up the grades it is very important to comment on these techniques and why they are used. The more consideration you can give to poetic technique, the more likely you are to score well. Remember, however, that it is important to keep the key term of the question in focus.

Look at this extract from a Band 4 response:

> The poet's feelings about nature are clear in the first line of the poem – 'Earth has not anything to show more fair ...' Wordsworth, as a Romantic poet, was well-known for his appreciation of the beauty of nature and so the reader wonders what aspect of nature he is praising so highly. It comes as a surprise then that he is praising the beauty of a city – London – and we can tell that the poet himself is surprised by the beauty he sees around him. The use of enjambment as he describes the city in front of him creates an effect of almost breathless amazement at what he sees, while the caesura in line 5 gives him the opportunity to pause and take in the view. This is followed by the long drawn out syllable of 'silent' which slows the pace and emphasises the peaceful beauty of the sleeping city.
>
> The personification of the city – 'The City now doth like a garment wear', 'And all that mighty heart is lying still' – gives the impression of something impressive, yet calm, while we can see that the city is not in conflict with the countryside, but almost part of it. 'Open unto the fields, and to the sky'.

- Addresses key term of question.
- Brief, but relevant, contextual information.
- Sustains discussion of poetic techniques.

Here we can see a concentrated effort to discuss the effects of the poetic technique which has been tied in to the key term of the question.

Review

Let's review some of the key words and ideas for this poem:

- **sonnet**
- **octave**
- **sestet**
- **personification**
- **enjambment**
- **caesura**.

Make sure you understand each term clearly. Make a list of definitions which you can use for revision.

'The Badger' by John Clare

Context
John Clare was a farm labourer who gained temporary fame as a poet. Later in life he suffered prolonged mental illness caused by financial difficulties, and perhaps by being abandoned by those who had praised him in his days of fame. His nature poetry is full of accurately observed details. In 'The Badger' he gives us a highly realistic picture of some aspects of English village life, its rowdiness and cruelty. He chose deliberately to write in his own language and dialect, in spite of the efforts of friends and publishers who wanted to correct his spelling and punctuation. The poem that you study is probably a corrected version.

ACTIVITY 20
Understanding the poem

1. How do the men catch the badger?
2. Make a list of the animals mentioned in this poem, and a brief note of the part played by each.
3. Referring to the poem, show how the poet conveys the noise and confusion of these events through the **use of detail** (both sight and sound).
4. What do you think is added to the poem by Clare's unusual spelling and language?
5. Clare introduces 'the old grunting badger' at the start of the poem, and then builds up a picture of the animal. List the words and phrases used and then write a descriptive paragraph about the animal and the part he plays in events.
6. How would you describe the villagers' treatment of animals in general, and the badger in particular? Give reasons for your opinions.

Moving up the grades

This is part of a Band 3 response to a question with the key term **feelings about nature**. This is not the only question that could be asked on this poem. Read the question on your examination paper carefully

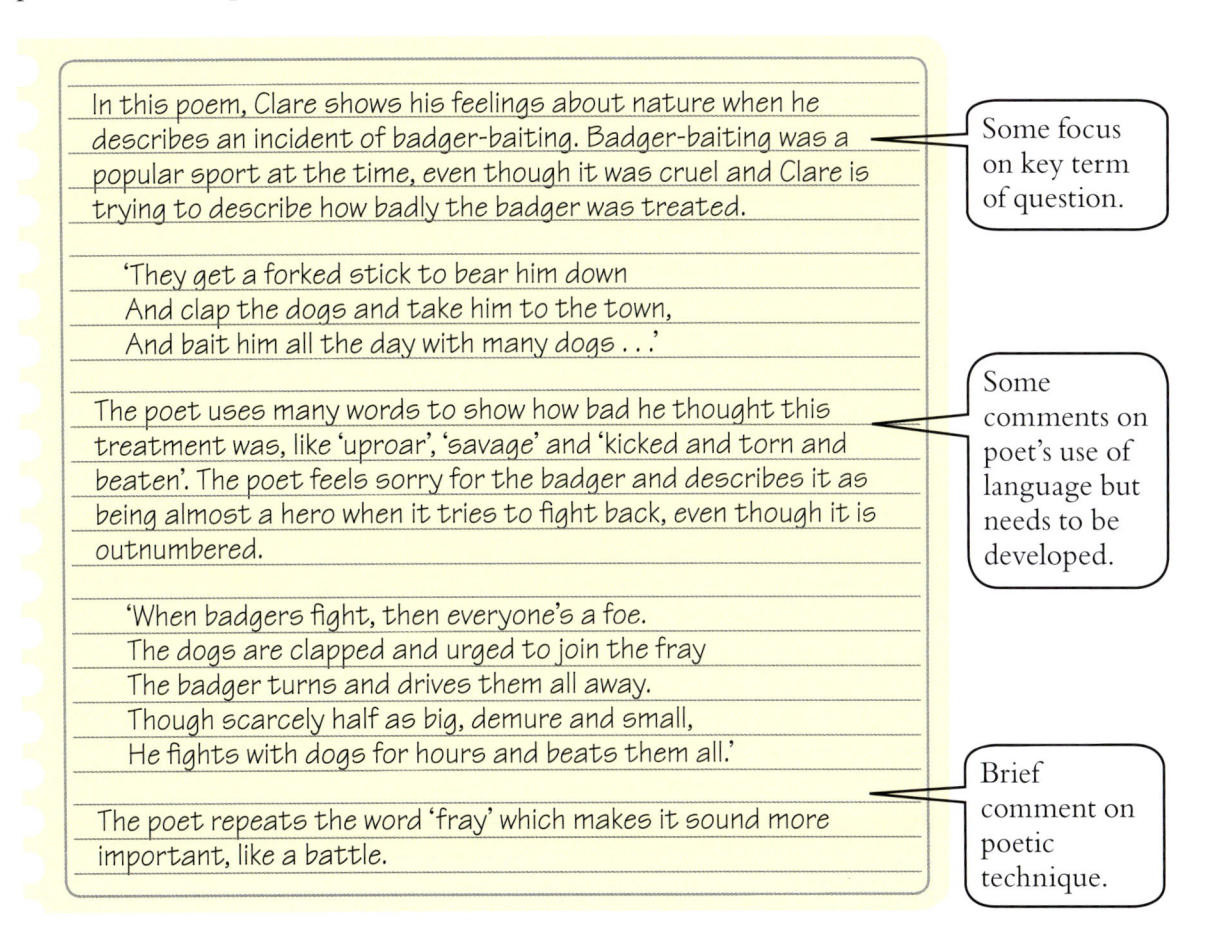

> In this poem, Clare shows his feelings about nature when he describes an incident of badger-baiting. Badger-baiting was a popular sport at the time, even though it was cruel and Clare is trying to describe how badly the badger was treated. [*Some focus on key term of question.*]
>
> 'They get a forked stick to bear him down
> And clap the dogs and take him to the town,
> And bait him all the day with many dogs …'
>
> The poet uses many words to show how bad he thought this treatment was, like 'uproar', 'savage' and 'kicked and torn and beaten'. The poet feels sorry for the badger and describes it as being almost a hero when it tries to fight back, even though it is outnumbered. [*Some comments on poet's use of language but needs to be developed.*]
>
> 'When badgers fight, then everyone's a foe.
> The dogs are clapped and urged to join the fray
> The badger turns and drives them all away.
> Though scarcely half as big, demure and small,
> He fights with dogs for hours and beats them all.'
>
> The poet repeats the word 'fray' which makes it sound more important, like a battle. [*Brief comment on poetic technique.*]

This response tries to focus on the speaker's **feelings about nature** and comments on the poet's use of language but it is undeveloped. The student could go on to speculate about the poet's use of language – does the term 'blackguard' refer to the badger or the village ne'er-do-well? If Clare is referring to the badger, what is the effect of this description?

Review

Let's review some of the key words and ideas for this poem:

- **repetition**
- **use of detail**
- **realism**.

Make sure you understand each term clearly. Make a list of definitions which you can use for revision.

'The Castle' by Edwin Muir

> **Context**
> Edwin Muir was a Scottish poet, born in the Orkney Islands. He became greatly interested in the interpretation of dreams. The **allegorical** poem 'The Castle' can be understood in several ways – personal or political, or just as a story in its own right.

ACTIVITY 21
Understanding the poem

1. Reread the first three verses and write a description of the actions and attitudes of the defenders. Refer to the words of the poem.
2. What is the effect of the use of run-on lines (enjambment) in verse 1?
3. What is the effect of the use of repetition in verse 2?
4. Where would you place the turning point of the poem?
5. Two **rhetorical questions** are used in the poem (at lines 16 and 26), but the tone in each is very different. Describe the tone of each. (The second response, opposite, includes possible responses.)
6. The poet makes use of sound effects in lines 18–20 – repetition and **alliteration**. What is the effect of these?
7. Why is the tale 'shameful'? Should we believe the speaker when he says 'we could do nothing'?
8. What, if anything, does the castle **symbolise**? Give reasons for your opinions.

Moving up the grades

This is an extract from a Band 2 response to Question 5 above.

> On line 16 it says 'What could they offer us for bait?' This is a rhetorical question which shows the reader that the people inside the castle don't think they can be beaten. But on line 26 it says 'How can this shameful tale be told?' This shows that the speaker is embarrassed that they were beaten in their castle.

This is a very limited response which does not make the most of the opportunity to refer to tone. It basically describes and offers a very simple statement about what the student thinks the lines mean. It is not enough simply to identify technique (in this case, rhetorical questions). If you wish to move up the grades, you need to think carefully about why the poet has used such techniques and comment on their effects.

The next extract makes a better attempt to discuss the poet's use of tone:

> In line 16, the rhetorical question 'What could they offer us for bait?' gives the speaker a tone of almost arrogance. Their castle seems impenetrable and they can exist safely inside, but more than this the speaker is complacent – the question implies that everyone inside is trustworthy and immune from temptation, which is shown by the use of word – 'bait'. However, the tone changes and the rhetorical question on line 26 – 'How can this shameful tale be told?' shows the speaker's embarrassment at what happened. The speaker wonders how he can admit the humiliation at their defeat in such a devious way – their pride in their 'famous citadel' was brought down by greed – 'our only enemy was gold'.

This student has made some attempt to analyse the tone created by the rhetorical questions in the poem. There are meaningful comments on use of language which support the points made about tone.

Review

Let's review some of the key words and ideas for this poem:

- **allegorical**
- **metaphor**
- **enjambment**
- **rhetorical question**
- **alliteration**
- **rhyme scheme**
- **symbol**.

Make sure you understand each term clearly. Make a list of definitions which you can use for revision.

'In Westminster Abbey' by John Betjeman

> **Context**
> In **satire** bad or foolish behaviour is made fun of in an attempt to correct it. This satirical poem is set in wartime London, and the behaviour targeted is the selfishness and hypocrisy of some upper-class people at that time.

ACTIVITY 22

Understanding the poem

1. The speaker expresses some shocking attitudes in verses 2 and 3. What are they?
2. This poem is a prayer, a direct address to God. How would you describe the **tone** of the speaker? Is it appropriate? Refer to the poem in your answer.
3. In verse 3 the lady shows what her country means to her. What is the poet mocking in this description?
4. There are several words and phrases in the poem that suggest the period in which the poem is set. List some of them.
5. Comment on the last two lines of the poem.
6. The poem is written in the language of prayer and the verse form is that of church hymns. Does this make the poem more enjoyable and effective? Give reasons for your answer.

Moving up the grades

This is part of a Band 3 response to a question with the key term **attitudes to war**. This is not the only question that could be asked on this poem. Read the question on your examination paper carefully.

> *Begins to focus on key term **attitudes to war**.*
>
> The speaker in this poem shows a very selfish attitude to war. Although she is supposed to be praying, her prayer is not very Christian.
>
> 'Gracious Lord, oh bomb the Germans . . .
> But, gracious Lord, whate'er shall be,
> Don't let anyone bomb me.'

> *Some understanding of language used.*
>
> Her selfish attitude is also shown when she asks God to 'protect the whites' while she is quite patronising about the foreign soldiers who fought in the war. And then she even gives her address to God as if God should pick out her house to protect it especially.

> 'Lord, put beneath Thy special care
> One-eighty-nine Cadogan Square.'

She lives in a very posh part of London, in Chelsea, so we can see that she represents a certain section of society – the snobs and hypocrites who are only looking out for themselves. She is not interested in the welfare of the soldiers but seems to want to make bargains with God to make sure she stays safe.

> 'I will labour for Thy Kingdom …
> Then wash the steps around Thy Throne
> In the Eternal Safety Zone.'

The contemptuous tone, especially in the final stanza, clearly shows what Betjeman thought about this type of person. She is shown to be so full of herself by the words:

> 'Now I feel a little better,
> What a treat to hear Thy word,
> Where the bones of leading statesmen,
> Have so often been interr'd.'

It seems that she is more interested in being seen praying in somewhere important like Westminster Abbey – doing her duty for the nation as she sees it – rather than any interest in faith. This is supported by the final couplet –

> 'And now, dear Lord, I cannot wait
> Because I have a luncheon date.'

Brief contextual detail.

Comments on tone – needs to be linked clearly with key term of question.

This response begins to focus on the key term of the question but it drifts off into a more general approach to the poem. There are some comments on poetic technique but they need to be more clearly linked to the question to move up the Mark Bands.

Review

Let's review some of the key words and ideas for this poem:

- **satire**
- **tone**
- **use of speaker**.

Make sure you understand each term clearly. Make a list of definitions which you can use for revision.

'The Battle' by Louis Simpson

Context
Louis Simpson served as a paratrooper in the US Army in Europe during the Second World War. Many of his early poems reflect his wartime experiences.

ACTIVITY 23

Understanding the poem

1. The figure of speech where a part represents the whole is called **synecdoche**. Note the use of this figure of speech in the first sentence. What is the effect on the reader?
2. What is the effect of the throat **simile** describing the night? Why is the night 'turning red'?
3. What methods does the poet use in lines 1–8 to describe the soldiers as unheroic?
4. Discuss the uses of **onomatopoeia** in the poem.
5. The cigarette image that ends the poem is the speaker's clearest memory of the battle. Referring closely to the poem, explain why this should be so.
6. What impressions of the experience of battle have you received from this poem?

Moving up the grades

These responses compare and contrast 'The Battle' and 'Attack' by Siegfried Sassoon.

This is part of a Band 2 response:

Refers to poet's words but at basic level.

Identifies poetic technique but makes no comment – a wasted opportunity!

> Simpson describes the way the soldiers are marching as they are being attacked. You can imagine what it was like for the soldiers because he says 'Their feet began to freeze'. He also uses a simile 'They sank like moles'.
>
> Sassoon describes the soldiers when they are getting ready to take part in an attack during the First World War. The soldiers are afraid because it says 'faces, masked with fear'. I like this poem better because you can imagine how scared the soldiers were.

Very simplistic personal response offered – more thought is needed here.

This response is very basic. The student simply picks out some words and adds basic remarks. There is little point in identifying poetic techniques without going on to explain or discuss the effects created by the poet's use of such techniques. Also the student has not made any attempt to compare or contrast the poems, which limits the marks.

A Band 4 response will take the opportunity to discuss the similarities and differences between the poems, for example:

> Both poets give the reader vivid images of the reality of war for the soldiers they describe. For example they both describe how the soldiers had to go into battle, laden down with kit. Simpson starts his poem, not by mentioning the soldiers but their kit:
>
> 'Helmet and rifle, pack and overcoat
> Marched through a forest.'
>
> This seems to be quite impersonal – as if the soldiers are not human, which could reflect the feelings of soldiers who had to suffer such dreadful conditions. Sassoon, describing First World War soldiers, does something similar:
>
> 'clumsily bowed
> With bombs and guns and shovels and battle-gear.'
>
> The repetition of 'and' emphasises the weight the soldiers had to carry while faced with bombardment from the enemy. This helps increase the reader's sympathy for these poor men.
>
> Another similarity between the poems is the change in tone, from almost narrative description of the scene in front of the speaker to a personal reaction to events. Sassoon's poem ends with a desperate cry 'O Jesus, make it stop!' which suddenly makes the reader realise the suffering of the soldiers. Simpson too moves from description to relating a personal memory – moving from 'They' to 'I'. This has the effect of making the battle more real to the reader as the speaker explains the lingering memory of 'tiredness in eyes, how hands looked thin . . . and the bright ember/ Would pulse with all the life there was within.' This final image reminds the reader of how fragile life is for these soldiers and is more shocking in my opinion than the early description of guns, shells and bullets.

- Responds to opportunities to make comparisons.
- Interprets meaning.
- Comments on effects of poetic technique.
- Personal response is embedded in answer.

This student makes some interesting connections between the poems and develops the points with carefully selected reference to the texts. The personal response to the poems is integrated into the answer, rather than tacked on at the end. This is a good skill to develop.

Review

Let's review some of the key words and ideas for this poem:

- **synecdoche**
- **onomatopoeia**
- **simile**.

Make sure you understand each term clearly. Make a list of definitions which you can use for revision.

'Death of a Naturalist' by Seamus Heaney

> **Context**
> In his early poems Seamus Heaney wrote a lot about his childhood on a farm – the buildings, the landscape, the people and the activities that made up an Ulster childhood in the 1940s and 1950s.

ACTIVITY 24

Understanding the poem

1 What are the sounds of the flax-dam, described near the beginning of the poem? What sound effects are used by the poet?

2 What does the figure of speech 'clotted water' mean?

3 How does the account of the school nature lesson show how young the pupils of Miss Walls were?

4 The poem is structured in two parts. Write a sentence for each part, showing what is dealt with. (The sample opposite includes a possible response.)

5 'Some hopped:/ The slap and plop were obscene threats' – comment on the sound effects used here.

6 How do the language and **imagery** (visual and aural) in the second part of the poem create an atmosphere of menace?

7 At times there is an underlying feeling of disgust in the poem. Pick out some of the words and phrases that represent this. What causes the disgust?

8 Why is the poem called 'Death of a Naturalist'?

Moving up the grades

This is part of a Band 3 response to a question with the key term **changing feelings about nature**. This is not the only question that could be asked on this poem. Read the question on your examination paper carefully.

> The poem's structure shows the speaker's changing feelings about nature. In the first part, the child is excited by nature and exploring the flax-dam. The childish words 'But best of all' show the child's enthusiasm for nature. The way the frogspawn is described appeals to the senses 'clotted . . . jellied'.
>
> However this childish enjoyment of nature is lost in the second part, where the speaker returns to the dam and is horrified by the 'gross-bellied frogs'. The way the frogs are described reflects the speaker's disgust and fear: 'obscene threats', 'poised like mud grenades'. The speaker is now afraid of being punished for taking the frogspawn and it seems that it isn't an adventure any more.
>
> 'I knew
> That if I dipped my hand the spawn would clutch it'.
>
> The first part appeals to the senses but the descriptions in the second part repel the senses – the speaker describes disgusting sounds like 'bass chorus' and 'farting'.

*Some focus on key term **changing feelings about nature**.*

Some comments on use of language and structure.

This student makes some valid comments on structure and use of language. They have missed the opportunity, however, to discuss the poet's use of imagery and other techniques.

Review

Let's review some of the key words and ideas for this poem:

- **onomatopoeia**
- **alliteration**
- **imagery** – **metaphor** and **simile**.

Make sure you understand each term clearly. Make a list of definitions which you can use for revision.

'A Narrow Fellow in the Grass' by Emily Dickinson

Context
Emily Dickinson wrote: 'To live is so startling, it leaves but little room for other occupations', and she herself lived a reclusive life. This poem records the intensity of the experience of encountering a snake while out walking.

ACTIVITY 25

Understanding the poem

1 This poem is rather like a riddle, in that it describes the creature without ever using the word 'snake'. Discuss the terms and images used for the snake.

2 The 'suddenness' of the snake's notice is mentioned in verse 1. How is this idea carried on through the poem?

3 Why do you think the idea of the boy being 'barefoot' is given in the poem? A boy, not a girl is the speaker. Why might the poet have made this choice?

4 Emily Dickinson's **punctuation** is often unusual. Do you think it adds anything to this poem?

5 The final verse of the poem deals with the reactions of the speaker on meeting the snake. What do you think is meant by the phrase 'Zero at the Bone'?

Moving up the grades

These responses compare and contrast 'A Narrow Fellow in the Grass' and 'The Badger' by John Clare. This is part of a Band 2 response:

Very basic reference to similarity.

Both these poems are about nature. In Dickinson's poem, she describes a snake and how it moves through the grass. The speaker doesn't seem to be afraid of the snake until the last stanza when she says

'But never met this fellow,
Attended or alone,
Without a tighter breathing'

Describes content of poems.

In 'The Badger' by John Clare the speaker describes a badger that is being hunted by people and dogs who want to use it for badger baiting which is a cruel sport. The speaker describes how the badger tries to fight back but is beaten and killed.

This student is aware of what the poems are about but will have difficulty scoring marks in the higher bands. Basic descriptions of content are not enough.

A better response (Band 4) will focus on use of language and poetic technique, for example:

> While Clare's poem is obviously about a badger from the title, Dickinson never mentions the word 'snake' in her poem. The reader can tell the poem is about a snake by Dickinson's clever descriptive techniques, for example the way she describes the snake's movement in the simile 'The grass divides as with a comb'. This helps the reader picture the image clearly. Even the layout of the poem seems to be trying to create the shape of the snake as it moves. The speaker seems to be very respectful of nature as the tone is one of admiration for the snake.
>
> This is similar to John Clare's poem where he describes the badger almost like a hero.
>
>   'The badger turns and drives them all away.
>   Though scarcely half as big, demure and small,
>   He fights with dogs for hours and beats them all.'
>
> Again, the tone here is one of admiration – the badger fights back even though it is outnumbered and tortured. Clare personifies the badger 'The badger grins' which shows Clare's admiration for this creature which is being cruelly treated for sport.

(Annotations: Comments on poetic techniques. Responds to opportunities for comparison. Comments on poetic techniques.)

This student makes some useful comparisons between the poems by looking at tone. There is some carefully selected reference to the poems to support the points made.

Review

Let's review some of the key words and ideas for this poem:

- **simile**
- **assonance**
- **punctuation**.

Make sure you understand each term clearly. Make a list of definitions which you can use for revision.

'Foxes among the Lambs' by Ernest Moll

> **Context**
> This autobiographical poem is drawn from the poet's experience as a sheep farmer in Australia. The Australian setting explains one or two details, such as 'the rainy south'.

ACTIVITY 26

Understanding the poem

1 What phrases at the beginning of the verses show that these events and emotions were repeated?
2 How does the poet convey the violence of the farmer's reaction to the death of his lambs in verse 1?
3 The farmer's emotions, described in verse 2, are violent but mixed. Write out the phrase that describes what he feels, and suggest an explanation for each of the emotions mentioned.
4 What is the effect of the succession of 'ands' at the end of verse 2?
5 In verse 1 the **imagery** is mainly **visual**; in verse 3 it is mainly **aural**. Give examples of each type of imagery and suggest a reason why the poet makes this change.
6 Comment on the last line of the poem.

Moving up the grades

This is part of a good Band 3 response to a question with the key term **cruelty in nature**. This is not the only question that could be asked on this poem. Read the question on your examination paper carefully.

> The poet shows how there is cruelty in nature, especially in the first stanza. The description of the fox attack on the lambs is gory and you can imagine what the farmer saw.
>
> 'Each morning there were lambs with bloody mouth,
> Their tongue cut out by foxes.'
>
> The horror of this description is added to by the account of how the farmer had to put the injured lambs down. Although the farmer's 'heart was sick' he describes having to 'smash their heads in with a handy stick'. This sounds cruel but that is what life is like on a farm.
>
> Cruelty is also shown when the farmer puts down poison for the foxes. It may seem brutal, but to protect his livestock, the farmer has to kill the foxes. The speaker describes his reactions to having to set the traps
>
> 'And I remember how my fingers shook
> With the half-frightened eagerness of hate'
>
> I think this shows that the farmer is aware that what he is doing is cruel because the farmer is shaking as he sets the trap. He can't sleep as he waits for the foxes to take the bait and we can imagine the cruel death at the end of the last stanza.
>
> 'While something in me waited for the leap
> Of a wild cry with death and terror in it;'

*Some focus on key term **cruelty in nature**.*

Comments on use of language.

Brief but relevant contextual detail.

Attempts an argument – not entirely convincing.

This student focuses on the key term and repeats it throughout. Some points are not developed fully and need more consideration. There are some valid comments about the poet's use of language which are worthy of credit.

Review

Let's review some of the key words and ideas for this poem:
- **visual and aural imagery**
- **rhyme scheme**
- **repetition**.

Make sure you understand each term clearly. Make a list of definitions which you can use for revision.

Unit 2 Section B: Poetry

Assessment Matrix – Higher Tier Unit 2 – Section B: Poetry

Assessment Objective	Band 0 Mark [0]	Band 1: Very Little [1]–[10]	Band 2: Emerging [11]–[18]	Band 3: Competent [19]–[26]	Band 4: Good [27]–[34]	Band 5: Excellent [35]–[40]
AO1 Argument	Response not worthy of credit	Some writing about text or task Very basic level of accuracy in written expression and coherence of response. Form mostly appropriate	Attempt to focus on content Simple, straightforward, or limited response Assertion, basic conclusion, narrative or description, quotation and/or paraphrase Fairly sound level of accuracy in written expression and coherence of response. Form mostly appropriate	Begins to focus on relevant content Begins to develop a response Some argument Competent level of accuracy in written expression and coherence of response. Form mostly appropriate	Sustained focus on relevant content Reasoned response Developed argument An appropriate form of response which is clearly constructed and accurately expressed	Persuasive, coherent answer to the question set Evaluative response Sustained argument An appropriate form of response which is clearly constructed and expressed with fluency and precision

146

AO2 **Form and Language**	Response not worthy of credit	Simplistic remarks about content Little or no awareness of structure, form or poetic techniques	Some awareness of content Some awareness of structure, form or poetic techniques Occasional reference to poet's words	Comments on content Explains structure, form or poetic technique Some understanding of the poet's use of language	Interpretation of content Comments on the effects of structure, form or poetic techniques Comments on language and style, with the emergence of a critical vocabulary	Assured interpretation of content Discussion on the effects of structure, form or poetic techniques Analysis of the poet's language and style, using appropriate critical terminology
AO3 **Comparison and Contrast**	Response not worthy of credit	Poems considered in isolation	Simple connections made between poems	Makes obvious comparisons and contrasts between poems	Responds to opportunities to compare and contrast poems	A synthesised approach to detailed comparison and contrast
AO4 **Awareness of Context**	Response not worthy of credit	No contextual material	Contextual material is present though not incorporated in argument	Some attempt to incorporate contextual material in argument	Selective use of contextual material to enhance argument	Response is enriched by use of contextual material

Anthology 3: Seamus Heaney and Thomas Hardy

'Thatcher' by Seamus Heaney

> **Context**
> Traditional crafts such as thatching survived in Ulster long into the twentieth century.

ACTIVITY 27

Understanding the poem

1. Clearly this craftsman was both independent and in demand. Which words and phrases convey this?
2. After the long series of actions (list them) why do you think the speaker comments 'It seemed he spent the morning warming up.'
3. Explain what is meant by the two **metaphors** ('staple' and 'world') in verse 2.
4. The word 'couchant' means 'lying', but is a much grander and more impressive word. Why do you think it is used to describe the workman lying on the roof?
5. In a metaphor, the thatched roof is compared to a 'sloped honeycomb'. Explain how this visual image is accurate.
6. The onlookers gaped at the thatcher's 'Midas touch'. What does this phrase mean and why is it appropriate?

Moving up the grades

This is part of a mid Band 3 response to a question with the key term **rural life in the past**. This is not the only question that could be asked on this poem. Read the question on your examination paper carefully.

Identifies poetic technique.

> Heaney gives us a great impression of the job of this man by listing all the tools of his trade. There is a ladder and knives and different kinds of twigs 'hazel and willow'. He arrives by bicycle, not in a van as you would expect a workman to do nowadays and Heaney says it was 'unexpectedly' so I assume they didn't have a telephone in the house in the 1940's. You wouldn't often see a man on a bike carrying a ladder nowadays either, because of the traffic. He may be a bit of a showman because it says 'he spent the morning warming up'. They say this to describe musicians getting ready to give their performance, and we know there was an audience for this man as 'he left them gasping at his Midas touch'. This is in my opinion the best metaphor in the poem. Midas was a king in ancient times (legend) who had the touch of gold. This compares with the thatcher who had the talent to make a beautiful golden roof out of a lot of dirty old straw. The honeycomb is also a good image, if you see the straw end on.

Discusses implications of word choice.

Comments on poetic technique.

Needs to say more to explain 'honeycomb' image. There is a missed opportunity here.

This is an observant student who has noticed several interesting and relevant features of the poem and is alert to what particular words may imply. There is comment on the use of language (though it is not always developed) and some focus on the question.

Examiner's tip!
Focus on the question. Use the key terms.

Review

Let's review some of the key words and ideas for this poem:

- **metaphor**
- **half-rhyme**
- **onomatopoeia**.

Make sure you understand each term clearly. Make a list of definitions which you can use for revision.

'Blackberry Picking' by Seamus Heaney

> **Context**
> Look up the story of Bluebeard in order to deepen your understanding of this poem.

ACTIVITY 28
Understanding the poem

1 'Its flesh was sweet/ Like thickened wine.' Which sense or senses does this simile appeal to?
2 'Summer's blood was in it.' Where is the idea of blood taken up again in the poem?
3 How is the energy and determination of the young blackberry pickers conveyed in lines 9–12?
4 What do the words 'hoarded' and 'cache' suggest about the children's attitude to what they have picked?
5 In the second section of the poem, which words and images convey disgust as the fruit 'goes off'. (The sample below gives a possible response.)
6 There are two cases of **full rhyme** in the poem. What effect on the reader does the poet wish to produce by using it?

Moving up the grades

This is a sample answer to Question 5 above:

Pays attention to poet's choice of words throughout.

Useful contextual reference.

Develops answer to include sound as well as visual imagery.

Shapes discussion and finishes off with general overview of topic.

> Although the children think they have found treasure, and the use of the word 'hoarded' shows this, their blackberries soon turn into something very unpleasant. The first ugly note is struck with the mention of 'fur' to describe the mould that began to grow on the fruit. 'Fur' is a word from the animal kingdom and is out of place here. In the next line we read of a 'rat-grey' fungus and connect the fur with rats, which provides a disgusting image. (We already know, from 'An Advancement of Learning' that Heaney was disgusted by rats and afraid of them, so this image is significant.) The sounds in the phrase that describes the way the fungus was eating the fruit, 'glutting on our cache', particularly the gl- and sh- sounds, are an unpleasant combination, and the choice of the word 'glutting' suggests disgusting gorging. Heaney's use of the word 'stinking' reinforces the disgust. The words 'sour' and 'rot' finish off the description, and there is an effective use of contrast in the placing of the word 'lovely' in the middle of the line 'all the lovely canfuls smelt of rot'. This description has appealed to the senses of sight, sound and taste (as 'sweet' becomes 'sour'.).

This is a Band 5 response with sustained argument and a developed discussion of the effects of poetic techniques.

Review

Let's review some of the key words and ideas for this poem:

- **metaphor**
- **sound values**
- **full rhyme**
- **near rhyme**.

Make sure you understand each term clearly. Make a list of definitions which you can use for revision.

Anthology 3: Heaney and Hardy

'At a Potato Digging' by Seamus Heaney

> **Context**
> The Irish potato famine (The Great Famine) happened in the 1840s.

ACTIVITY 29
Understanding the poem

1. Look at the verbs in the first two sentences. What do they convey about the activity that is going on?
2. Look at the **simile** at the start of verse 2. In what ways are the labourers like crows?
3. What comparison is being made when the workers 'stumble back/ To fish a new load from the crumbled surf'? Does the word 'creel' add to this?
4. The poem begins with a piece of modern machinery but ends in a very different way. List the religious terms used near the end of the poem. What thoughts about the potato digging is the speaker expressing?
5. List in order the things the labourers are compared to. Note down the instances where they are referred to by a part of the body and try to suggest a reason for this.

Moving up the grades

For these responses, the key term was **rural life**. This is not the only question that could be asked on this poem. Read the question on your examination paper carefully.

This is part of a Band 2 response. This student chose to compare and contrast 'At a Potato Digging' with 'A Sheep Fair'.

Attempts to focus on question (but seems to want to write about work).

Some awareness of poetic technique. Refers to the poets' words.

> This poem describes the work done in the country. Here it is digging potatoes. We read how the 'mechanical digger wrecks the hill' and then afterwards the workmen come in to pick the potatoes. They put the potatoes into baskets called creels, not much used nowadays. They are described in the field like crows because there are so many of them and they are wearing black clothes. It is very cold and the poem says 'Their fingers go dead in the cold'.

Makes only simple connections between poems.

> I can compare this with Thomas Hardy's 'A Sheep Fair' because the work there is also very uncomfortable. The work is different because they are buying and selling cattle, but just as uncomfortable because of the rain. It is so wet even the sheep's horns have gone soft and the auctioneer 'wrings out his beard'.

This is part of a Band 4 response:

> Heaney makes use of synecdoche in describing the workmen. This is a figure of speech where a part of something stands for the whole thing. So here the workmen are referred to as 'trunks', 'heads' and 'hands'. This gives a strange effect as if we are only seeing a little bit of their bodies clearly as we do sometimes when we are very tired. Perhaps this is Heaney's intention....

Examiner's tip!
Focus on the question. Use the key terms.

This student has noticed a poetic technique and suggests what the effect of that technique might be. It would be a good idea to develop the idea of tiredness.

Review

Let's review some of the key words and ideas for this poem:

- **simile**
- **alliteration**
- **synecdoche**.

Make sure you understand each term clearly. Make a list of definitions which you can use for revision.

'Last Look' by Seamus Heaney

Context
The travelling shops of rural Ulster have still not quite died out, though now they are motorised. If you can find out something about the legend of Niamh and Oisín, it will deepen your understanding of the poem.

ACTIVITY 30

Understanding the poem

1 What details and images in the description of the old man suggest his absent-mindedness?

2 How is the world of the old man's memories made to seem realistic?

3 The final section of the poem works by suggesting something very far-fetched: 'If Niamh had ridden up. . .'. Look at the ending of the poem and suggest why the poet uses this far-fetched suggestion.

4 The language used to describe the arrival of Niamh is different from that in other parts of the poem. What does the poet intend to suggest by using this altered language?

5 What separate meanings might the title have?

Moving up the grades

This is part of a Band 3 response to a question with the key term **old age**. This is not the only question that could be asked on this poem. Read the question on your examination paper carefully.

> In 'Last Look' Heaney gives us a picture of an old man standing at the side of the road gazing into a potato field. He pays no attention to the speaker and he is 'oblivious' and 'pays no heed' This is very typical as when people are old they are often very absent-minded. 'He seemed not to hear' even though the speaker has come right up to him in a car.
>
> The old man is compared to 'sheep's wool on barbed wire' and 'an old lock of hay' to suggest to the reader that he is slightly untidy. We know this already from the detail of his trousers being wet and 'flecked with grass-seed'.
>
> The old man is described as staring and absent-minded because he is back in his memories. Again this is typical of old people who tend to live in the past. He is remembering the days when he took a horse and cart through Donegal to sell groceries round the farms. We can tell how long ago it was because there was a big drama if he met a car. The model of the car tells us that he was remembering the 1920s. The poet gives us other details of what that time was like – 'flourbags, nosebags, buckets of water'. The poem ends with an allusion to the legend of Oisin who suddenly became very old when Niamh sent him back to the world. The last line is a metaphor. Heaney says that he would not come out of the 'covert of his gaze'. A covert is where an animal hides and this old man is not easy to know.

Some focus on question.

Point not made clearly.

Identifies a few poetic techniques and comments on them briefly.

This response has some focus on the question. The student knows the poem fairly well and is able to make some simple comments about the poet's use of language. They begin to develop an argument, but more work could be done on several of the points touched on.

Review

Let's review some of the key words and ideas for this poem:

- **hyperbole**
- **imagery**
- **allusion**.

Make sure you understand each term clearly. Make a list of definitions which you can use for revision.

'An Advancement of Learning' by Seamus Heaney

> **Context**
> Several of Heaney's poems show his horror of rats when he was young.

ACTIVITY 31
Understanding the poem

1. The bridge is mentioned twice in the poem, in the first and last verses. There is also a 'bridgehead' halfway through. How does this reflect the speaker's changing attitude? Refer to the words of the poem.
2. How do the words and phrases used to describe the first rat help us to understand the speaker's 'sickened' feeling?
3. What does the word 'incredibly' tell us about the speaker's feelings at this point in the poem? Does the word 'thrilled' in the next verse mark a turning point in the poem? Give reasons for your answer.
4. Do the later descriptions of rats contain as much 'terror' as the first? Refer to the words and phrases of the poem.
5. What is your explanation of the title of the poem?

Moving up the grades

This is part of a borderline Band 3/4 response to a question with the key term **an encounter with an animal**. This is not the only question that could be asked on this poem. Read the question on your examination paper carefully.

Focuses on question.

Notes structure but does not develop point.

Comments on effect of poetic technique.

> The poem's title is clever and relevant (because the speaker does learn something from the encounter) but it does not prepare us for the horror of the encounter with the rat. The setting is a dirty river-bank in the city. Even the swans, usually so beautiful and graceful, are 'dirty-keeled' and the river is oily. Its 'transfer of colours' refers to the pollution in the water and compares the way it looks to the brightly coloured transfers worn by children. The rat comes in in verse three. 'Rat' is placed at the end of a line for emphasis and the speaker, who seems to be Heaney himself, describes its busy movements – 'nimbling', 'clockworked aimlessly'. Not just the sight is horrible, the sound is too and the effects on the speaker are severe. He feels sick in his throat and comes out in a 'cold sweat'.

Needs to develop these points, e.g. say something about the movements or give an illustration of the horrible sounds.

> The second description of the rat also has its horrible moments. By describing 'the tapered tail that followed him' the poet is letting us imagine that the tail has a life of its own. And 'the old snout' may mean that the rat he saw was old, but may also mean that the speaker and the rat have a long history and that he has been afraid of rats for a long time. This reminds me of the young Heaney's nightmare in 'The Barn'. This is backed up by the details of rats in the childhood home, where rats were very close 'on ceiling boards above my head'. In a kind of metaphor, the rat becomes an emotion, 'this terror . . .'.

Useful contextual reference.

What is backed up? Argument needs to be clearer.

Interprets subject matter.

This shows evidence of hard work in some respects but the response is also a little lazy in others. Developing the argument – for example, so as to discuss the differences between the two descriptions of rats – would ensure a higher mark band.

Review

Let's review some of the key words and ideas for this poem:

- **sound effects**
- **structure**
- **metaphor**
- **onomatopoeia**.

Make sure you understand each term clearly. Make a list of definitions which you can use for revision.

'Trout' by Seamus Heaney

> **Context**
> There was a fashion for poems describing animals in the 1960s and 1970s.

ACTIVITY 32
Understanding the poem

1. List the occasions where weapon imagery is used to describe the trout. What are the poet's intentions in describing the trout in this way?
2. The second verse describes the trout feeding. How are the accuracy and deadliness of the trout's attack suggested?
3. What sound effects are used when the trout is described jumping?
4. What is the effect of splitting the word 'tracer-bullet' with a line break?
5. What are the qualities of the trout which the poet singles out? For each quality you mention, provide a suitable quotation.

Moving up the grades

This is part of a Band 3 response to a question with the key term **ways of looking at nature**. This is not the only question that could be asked on this poem. Read the question on your examination paper carefully.

The student chose to compare and contrast 'Trout' with 'An August Midnight'.

> The speaker in Heaney's 'Trout' is not part of the action. In fact there is no action involving human beings, just the trout swimming and jumping and feeding, and the speaker describes it. The speaker in 'An August Midnight' also describes nature, but he is more involved and is disturbed by the insects.

Makes obvious connections between poems.

> From the start the trout is described as something powerful and dangerous, a gun-barrel and a tracer-bullet. It is expert at hitting its targets, which are its food (moths and grass-seed). The poet uses a metaphor here comparing the food to the bull's eye of a target. The insects in 'An August Midnight' are obviously not powerful and dangerous, but you get the impression they would be if they were bigger, because Hardy says they are 'winged, horned and spined'. Another thing about the trout is that it is slippery. The poet uses a simile to say that it 'slips like butter down the throat of the river'. The trout is powerful also because it comes up from the deep water quickly and suddenly and the grass-seeds and moths 'vanish torpedoed'. This gives the impression of a very sudden attack and the verse ends with the word 'torpedoed' and there is a pause before the next verse.
>
> Of these two poems the one which makes a bigger impression on me is 'An August Midnight' because the speaker is disturbed by these insects that fly in but he doesn't get angry even when they walk in his ink and spoil the work he is doing. But in Heaney's poem the speaker is just there watching and comparing and we don't get as good a picture of the kind of person he is.

Some understanding of poet's use of language.

Brief comment on poet's technique. Poor planning weakens this paragraph.

Explanation offered for student's preference but it is brief and underdeveloped.

This response could have moved further up Band 3 if the student had focused more explicitly on the key term of the question and planned and developed the points better. A good point is made in comparing and contrasting the poems but here too there could have been more development.

Examiner's tip!

Use the key term of the question.

Review

Let's review some of the key words and ideas for this poem:

- **metaphor**
- **simile**
- **onomatopoeia**.

Make sure you understand each term clearly. Make a list of definitions which you can use for revision.

'The Old Workman' by Thomas Hardy

> **Context**
> Thomas Hardy's father worked as a stonemason, and the poet knew not only the jargon but also the hardships of the trade. The reference to the old mason's 'life ache' reminds us that in the nineteenth century he would have received no incapacity benefits, but would have had to work on. This is a question-and-answer poem, though the mason's answer goes beyond the question asked.
>
> Hardy grew up in Dorset, at a time when that area was very remote. In his novels and in many of his poems he uses words of Dorset **dialect**.

ACTIVITY 33

Understanding the poem

1 List the stone-working terms used. What is the effect of using such technical terms in the poem?
2 The height of the work the mason was doing is emphasised several times. What is the purpose of the repetition?
3 What phrase conveys the soundness and lasting quality of the mason's work?
4 Comment on the poet's use of the words 'crack' and 'crookt'.
5 The phrase 'life's ache' suggests years of discomfort or pain. In a few sentences, describe the workman's attitude to living with his injury.

Moving up the grades

For these responses, the key term of the question was **a description of an old person**. This is not the only question that could be asked on this poem. Read the examination paper carefully.

This is part of a Band 2 response:

> The man described in Hardy's poem is a builder or a bricklayer. His work is very hard and he is 'bent down'. Later in the poem we read that he got a back injury carrying bricks up the scaffolding. He tells the story of the accident and how 'and something in my back moved as 'twere with a crack and I got crookt'. He doesn't mind thinking about the rich people living comfortably in the house he built...

Describes the man – this is an attempt to focus.

Try to lay out quotations correctly, and blend them into your sentence.

This is a limited, descriptive response. It refers to the poet's words, but does not comment on poetic technique. It gives only the most obvious facts about the workman – nothing about his attitude to his work and very little about his attitude to those who have been luckier than he has been. What about the key term **old**?

Here is part of a Band 3 response:

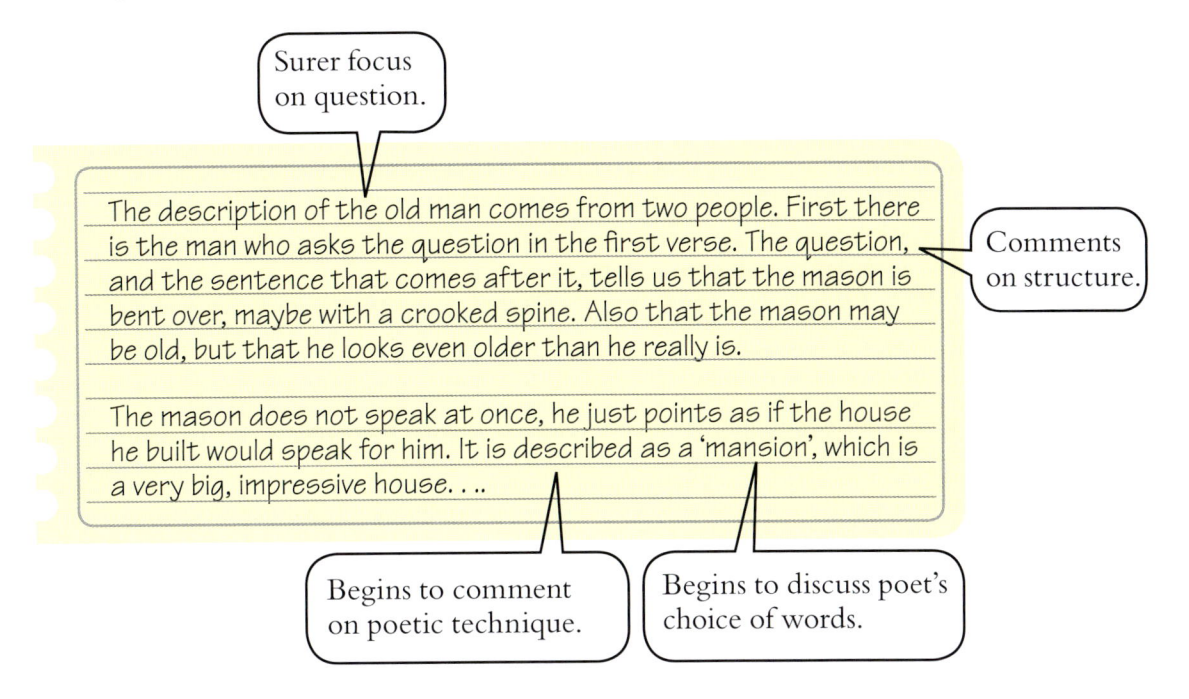

> *[Surer focus on question.]*
>
> The description of the old man comes from two people. First there is the man who asks the question in the first verse. The question, and the sentence that comes after it, tells us that the mason is bent over, maybe with a crooked spine. Also that the mason may be old, but that he looks even older than he really is.
>
> The mason does not speak at once, he just points as if the house he built would speak for him. It is described as a 'mansion', which is a very big, impressive house....

[Comments on structure.]

[Begins to comment on poetic technique.]

[Begins to discuss poet's choice of words.]

This opening is better than the Band 2 sample because it is beginning to do some things that can be rewarded: it is beginning to comment on structure, and to discuss the poet's use of language.

Review

Let's review some of the key words and ideas for this poem:

- **characterisation through dialogue**
- **rhyme scheme**
- **structure**
- **dialect**.

Make sure you understand each term clearly. Make a list of definitions which you can use for revision.

'Wagtail and Baby' by Thomas Hardy

Context
We prefer to build bridges nowadays and keep our feet and cars dry and clean, but in the nineteenth century fords at streams and rivers were common. Animals liked them as places to cool down on hot days.

ACTIVITY 34
Understanding the poem

1. The three animals that approach the ford are carefully chosen and described. What qualities do we associate with these animals, and how does the poet use language to suggest these qualities? (The sample below includes possible responses.)
2. What words and phrases are used to describe the movements of the wagtail as it drinks. What impressions do you get of the movements of the bird?
3. Is it significant that when a human approaches the ford, he is described as 'a perfect gentleman'? Give reasons for your opinions.
4. What key word is used to indicate the wagtail's reaction to the gentleman?
5. What do you think the baby was thinking about at the end of the poem?

Review

Let's review some of the key words and ideas for this poem:

- **contrast**
- **rhyme**
- **structure**.

Make sure you understand each term clearly. Make a list of definitions which you can use for revision.

Moving up the grades

This is a sample answer to Question 1 above.

> Hardy keeps up the interest of the reader by cleverly contrasting the animals that come to the ford before the 'perfect gentleman' arrives. Expressions such as 'Behaving like a bull in a china-shop' show how we think of bulls. They are large, noisy and dangerous animals that can do a lot of damage. Hardy chooses the perfect word – 'blaring' to describe it. It alliterates with 'bull', which makes the phrase pleasant to read and listen to. It is important in the poem that when faced with this huge and noisy creature, the little wagtail is not upset.
>
> The next animal to arrive is a stallion. Also big, powerful and dangerous. Stallions are worth thousands of pounds if they are thoroughbreds, and this one is, or thinks he is! Every word Hardy uses shows how arrogant this horse is. First he nearly drowns the wagtail. 'He gives his plumes a twitch and toss' as if he was some kind of diva! Plumes are the long, valuable feathers of a rare bird but just the right word for the mane of this proud creature. 'He held his own unblinking' – It is a shame there is only a little wagtail for him to stare out.
>
> The contrast with the noisy, rather stupid bull was great enough, but the third animal's arrival widens the contrast even further. If a stallion is a thoroughbred, a mongrel most definitely is not and Hardy again finds the perfect word to describe this sneaking, guilty-looking creature: 'slinking'. He observantly says the mongrel is sneaking 'round the spot'. It does not dare walk straight through the ford, but slinks round the edges.

- Focuses on the animals' qualities.
- Interprets character – note that this is backed up with reference to text.
- Develops argument about poetic technique of contrast.

This is a Band 4 response and, if the argument is sustained, will move into Band 5.

'A Sheep Fair' by Thomas Hardy

> **Context**
> The place names in Hardy's poems are often slightly changed versions of the names of real locations in Dorset.

ACTIVITY 35
Understanding the poem

1. In many of Hardy's poems he gives us surprising and unfamiliar details. Are there any such details in his description of a sheep fair?
2. A darker note is struck in the 'Postscript'. What poetic techniques does the poet use to do this?
3. The poem uses a very repetitive **rhyme scheme**. Suggest reasons why Hardy might have chosen to use it for the subject of this poem.
4. In what ways does the poet avoid monotony in the structure of his verses? (You will find some suggestions in the Review section opposite.)

Review

Let's review some of the key words and ideas for this poem:

- **rhyme scheme**
- **repetition**
- **use of long and short lines**
- **alliteration**
- **simile**.

Make sure you understand each term clearly. Make a list of definitions which you can use for revision.

Moving up the grades

This is part of a Band 3 response to a question with the key term **an unpleasant experience**. This is not the only question that could be asked on this poem. Read the examination paper carefully.

> The experience of Pummery Fair is an unpleasant one because of the rain. It always takes place on the same day and is a huge event with ten thousand sheep. The first verse describes the auctioneer and the day is certainly unpleasant for him. He just has to work through 'lot by lot'. Hardy gives us details that show us how unpleasant the day is for him. He has to wring out his beard he is so wet and so is his notebook, with the ink all smeared and his face streaming with the rain. Hardy uses a very repetitive rhyme scheme 'reared – cleared – beard – smeared' to suggest how monotonous and long-lasting the rain was.
>
> Verse two is about the sheep and the shepherds. For the sheep it really is unpleasant as they are so crowded 'jammed tight'. They can hardly move and 'their horns are as soft as finger-nails' with the wet. The shepherds are in wet clothes and they 'reek' which means they smell bad so that is another reason for it being an unpleasant experience. The sheep-dogs are tired with work. Hardy uses a very repetitive rhyme scheme again 'nails – rails – tails – pails' to suggest how monotonous the rain is.

Annotations:
- Description – repeats details of poem.
- Focuses on key term.
- Begins to comment on poetic technique, but the point has already been made. The student is short of things to say.

This response does focus on the question but it is mostly simple description. It just begins to comment on the rhyme scheme. This is a low Band 3 response.

'At Castle Boterel' by Thomas Hardy

> **Context**
> Hardy took care to date this poem March 1913: he was 72. It is one of a number of poems he wrote at that time about his late wife Emma. The passengers' reaction to the pony's complaining sigh takes us back to an era when driving involved horses.

ACTIVITY 36

Understanding the poem

1. Do the weather conditions in the first and last verses of the poem suit the speaker's mood? Give reasons for your opinion.
2. Does the speaker contradict himself in what he says about what he and the girl talked of? Give reasons for your answer.
3. How does the speaker indicate that the conversation he had with the girl was out of the ordinary?
4. What is the poet saying about time when he speaks of the 'hill's story' and the 'primaeval rocks'?
5. What does the speaker see now on the slope, and what is happening to the thing he sees?
6. Why does the poet give 'Time' a capital letter in verse 6 (though not elsewhere in the poem). Give reasons for your opinions.
7. Explain the **metaphor** 'my sand is sinking'.

Moving up the grades

This is part of a Band 4 response to a question with the key term **feelings about the past**. This is not the only question that could be asked on this poem. Read the examination paper carefully.

The student is comparing 'At Castle Boterel' with Seamus Heaney's 'Last Look'.

> While both the old man described in 'Last Look' and the speaker in 'At Castle Boterel' are remembering the past, what is remembered is very different, though both memories seem to be happy ones.
>
> It is just the place that causes the speaker to remember the long ago walk with the girl. He tells the story of how they got down from their cart to make it easy for the pony and walked up the hill. He seems to try to avoid saying that the experience was important: he says it 'mattered not much', but he may still find something painful in the memory. And the walk did lead on to something important, 'something that life will not be balked of'. This is an unusual word meaning life will not be prevented from having it. So perhaps marriage is meant.

(Focuses on question.)

(Brief quotations used correctly.)

> The speaker contrasts the short time the walk lasted with the quality of the experience and uses a rhetorical question which he answers himself, asking if the hill they were on had ever witnessed a 'time of such quality' and answering 'never'.
>
> Towards the end of the poem the speaker seems to be stretching time out. We know that he is remembering something from his own lifetime but when he uses the word 'primaeval' it seems as though he is speaking of millions of years ago. In the same way as time is stretched, so is space, and the speaker says, 'I look back and see it there shrinking, shrinking', and the repetition of shrinking and the rhyme on 'sinking' give a very sad effect at the end of the poem, which is made even sadder by the last two words 'Never again'.

Comments on effects of poetic technique.

This Band 4 response offers some relevant comments on language and style. Its final mark will depend on how well it solves the problem of the argument. In the first paragraph it seems to be argued that this is a happy memory but towards the end of the sample all the talk is of sadness. How would you sort this out?

Examiner's tip!

Make sure you **develop** your answer so as to get full value from the points you make.

Review

Let's review some of the key words and ideas for this poem:

- **metaphor**
- **personification**
- **rhyme**.

Make sure you understand each term clearly. Make a list of definitions which you can use for revision.

'An August Midnight' by Thomas Hardy

> **Context**
> Remember that Hardy would have been writing with a fountain pen, or even a dip pen. Hardy was fond of occasionally using **dialect** words in his poetry, such as the word 'Dumbledore'.

ACTIVITY 37

Understanding the poem

1. What is the **rhythm** of line 2 intended to suggest?
2. On several occasions the speaker refers to the insects as if they were people. Write out and discuss the lines where he does so.
3. Two attitudes to the insects in the room are suggested at the end of the poem. In your own words say what these two attitudes are.
4. 'Thus meet we five, in this still place,/ At this point of time, at this point in space.' The slow rhythm and the use of **repetition** in these lines suggest a solemn and important meeting. Is this appropriate or inappropriate? Give reasons for your opinions.

Moving up the grades

This is part of a Band 3 response to a question with the key term **feelings about nature**. This is not the only question that could be asked on this poem. Read the examination paper carefully.

> This is a very simple poem where four insects come into Hardy's work-room in the middle of the night and disturb him. The waving blind shows that the window is open and I suppose the insects came in through the window. They are described as 'winged horned and spined'. Hardy uses a metaphor to describe the fourth insect in the lines 'While 'mid my page there idly stands/ A sleepy fly that rubs its hands'. The metaphor compares the fly to a sleepy person.

Very simple comment on poetic technique.

> When he says 'Thus meet we five', it seems almost as if the five of them are five people there in the room. They walk over the page he has just written and smudge the ink but he is not angry. In the nineteenth century Hardy would have written with an old pen that you would have to use blotting paper with. So the ink was wet and could be smeared. At the end of the poem Hardy says that the insects are 'God's humblest'. That means that they are the simplest and least important life-form. But then he thinks again and decides that the insects are more important and know more than he does. This is true if you think of survival. Insects have survived longer than man. But there is a well-known phrase about being drawn like a moth to a candle and these insects bang at the lamp. In those days the lamp would have had a flame that would kill the moth.

Some awareness of context.

Good ideas relevant to key term of question, but not developed.

This is a response with some interesting and relevant ideas, but it only begins to develop them. There is some reference to the words of the poem, but the discussion of poetic technique does not go far enough to climb far into Band 3.

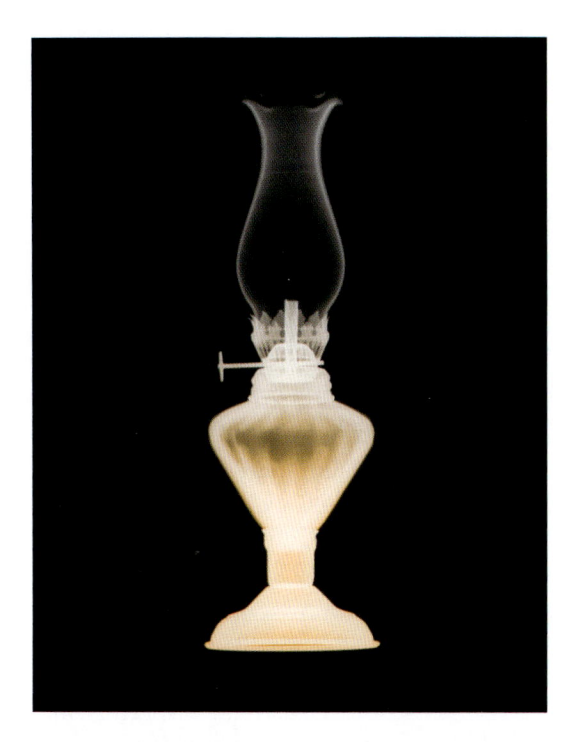

Review

Let's review some of the key words and ideas for this poem:

- **rhythm**
- **repetition**
- **dialect**.

Make sure you understand each term clearly. Make a list of definitions which you can use for revision.

'Overlooking the River Stour' by Thomas Hardy

> **Context**
> Another poem with a Dorset setting. The theme of missing something of emotional importance, happening sometimes in the same room, is found several times in Hardy's poetry.

ACTIVITY 38
Understanding the poem

1. What are the swallows and the moorhen compared to in the first two verses? Is there anything surprising in these comparisons? Give reasons for your opinions. (The sample below includes possible responses.)
2. The third verse shows a change in the weather. How has it changed and what words are used to describe it as it is now? Does the weather add to the impression the poem makes on the reader?
3. What are the feelings of the speaker expressed in the final verse? How are they suggested?
4. Does the unfinished sentence in the final verse add to the effectiveness of the poem? Give reasons for your opinions.

Moving up the grades

This is part of a Band 5 response to a question with the key term **natural surroundings**. This is not the only question that could be asked on this poem. Read the examination paper carefully.

The imagery used to describe the swallows flying over the surface of the river is very striking. We have all probably noticed that swallows fly in figure eights but I would never have thought of comparing these birds to 'little cross-bows animate'. This simile does describe the appearance in flight of these birds exactly though, as the curved shape of their wings is like the cross-piece of a cross-bow and the body is like the handle.

The surprising imagery continues in the second verse, using a metaphor this time to compare the moorhen taking off from the surface of the river with a wood-plane. The drops of water thrown off are like the light shavings of wood thrown to the side by the plane.

[Evaluative response.] The strange thing about the imagery in these two verses is the underlying violence. To compare an innocent bird to a deadly weapon is remarkable enough, but when the words 'ripped his way' are used to describe the moorhen on the water we may begin to wonder if there is some hidden violent emotion on the part of the speaker.

> The third verse is just as observant, but quieter. There are no similes or metaphors this time but the details of the meadow are described clearly – the closed flowers, the dripping grass – and contrasted with the earlier sunshine when the meadow was 'honeybee'd', a piece of wording characteristic of Hardy. The speaker is certainly attentive to the natural surroundings, but there seems to be something unexplained about his attitude to them. The phrase 'Dripped in monotonous green' is repeated, and the repetition used in the stanza form, along with the incantatory, limited rhyme scheme, has now created a tone of sadness to exist along with the violence we discussed earlier. In 'Overlooking the River Stour' the speaker's description of the natural surroundings is mysteriously charged with emotion.

Sustained argument.

This Band 5 response discusses the imagery in the first three verses of the poem. The discussion sustains its focus on the key term of the question: **natural surroundings**.

Examiner's tip!
Focus on the question. Use the key terms.

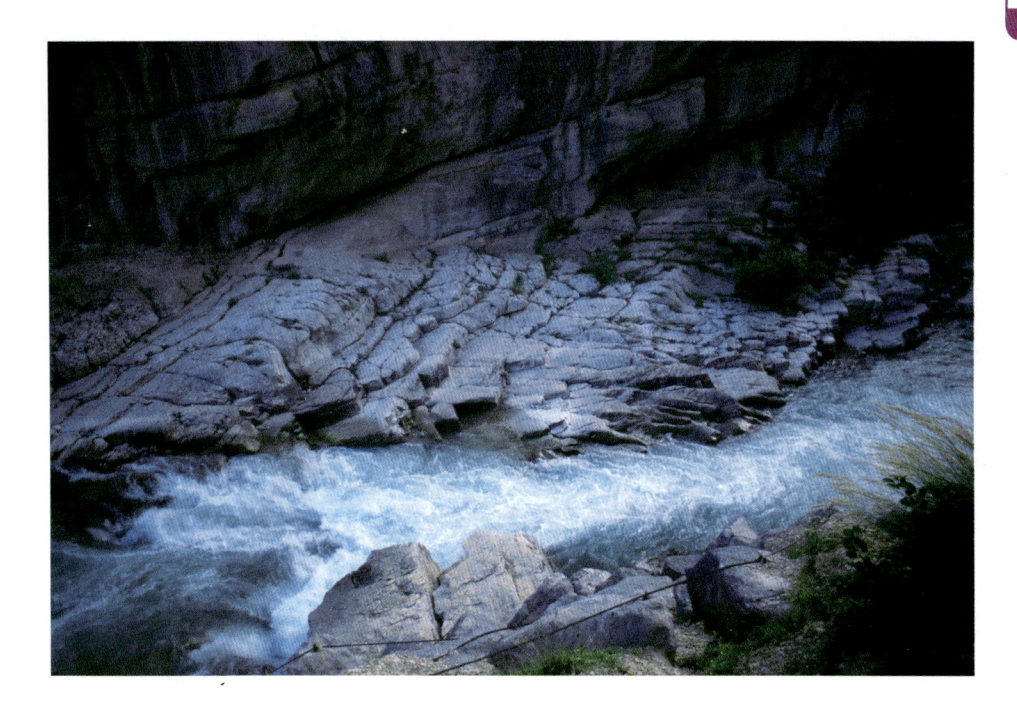

Review

Let's review some of the key words and ideas for this poem:

- **simile**
- **metaphor**
- **repetition**
- **stanza**.

Make sure you understand each term clearly. Make a list of definitions which you can use for revision.

Unit 2 Section B: Poetry

Assessment Matrix – Higher Tier Unit 2 – Section B: Poetry

Assessment Objective	Band 0 Mark [0]	Band 1: Very Little [1]–[10]	Band 2: Emerging [11]–[18]	Band 3: Competent [19]–[26]	Band 4: Good [27]–[34]	Band 5: Excellent [35]–[40]
AO1 Argument	Response not worthy of credit	Some writing about text or task Very basic level of accuracy in written expression and coherence of response. Form mostly appropriate	Attempt to focus on content Simple, straightforward, or limited response Assertion, basic conclusion, narrative or description, quotation and/or paraphrase Fairly sound level of accuracy in written expression and coherence of response. Form mostly appropriate	Begins to focus on relevant content Begins to develop a response Some argument Competent level of accuracy in written expression and coherence of response. Form mostly appropriate	Sustained focus on relevant content Reasoned response Developed argument An appropriate form of response which is clearly constructed and accurately expressed	Persuasive, coherent answer to the question set Evaluative response Sustained argument An appropriate form of response which is clearly constructed and expressed with fluency and precision

170

AO2 **Form and Language**	Response not worthy of credit	Simplistic remarks about content Little or no awareness of structure, form or poetic techniques	Some awareness of content Some awareness of structure, form or poetic techniques Occasional reference to poet's words	Comments on content Explains structure, form or poetic technique Some understanding of the poet's use of language	Interpretation of content Comments on the effects of structure, form or poetic techniques Comments on language and style, with the emergence of a critical vocabulary	Assured interpretation of content Discussion on the effects of structure, form or poetic techniques Analysis of the poet's language and style, using appropriate critical terminology
AO3 **Comparison and Contrast**	Response not worthy of credit	Poems considered in isolation	Simple connections made between poems	Makes obvious comparisons and contrasts between poems	Responds to opportunities to compare and contrast poems	A synthesised approach to detailed comparison and contrast
AO4 **Awareness of Context**	Response not worthy of credit	No contextual material	Contextual material is present though not incorporated in argument	Some attempt to incorporate contextual material in argument	Selective use of contextual material to enhance argument	Response is enriched by use of contextual material

Unit 2

The Study of Drama and Poetry
Section C: Unseen Poetry

Bringing it all together

Some reminders about the Unseen Poetry unit (Unit 2: Section C)

What is being assessed?
- Your understanding of an unseen poetry text
- Your understanding of the ways the poet uses language
- 'Quality of written communication'

Note: There are no marks available here for comparison of poems or for context.

The wording of the questions will stress the importance of considering the ways the poet uses language.

Time, planning and practice . . . and your attitude

You should spend **30 minutes** on the Unseen Poetry question. There will be **one** poem for you to write about.

It is most important that you **plan** your answer, especially at Higher tier, where the question is not divided into parts and there is less guidance. Not only is the question more structured at Foundation tier, the poem itself is likely to be more straightforward. You should consider this when deciding which tier to enter for.

Without planning, your answer is likely to be incoherent, so you should set aside some time for careful reading and **rereading**, and for deciding how to sequence and develop your material. Thirty minutes is the shortest time available for any of the questions in the examinations. The examiners will be realistic about what you can do in the time available.

You cannot revise for unseen material, but you can practise. You should practise dealing with unseen poems and managing the time available to you. You will find some practice tasks on pages 174–184. You can also use the poems in the two Anthologies that you are not studying for practice. These will give you experience of a range of styles, themes and poetic forms.

Setting aside time for careful reading, reflection and planning is essential. It is likely that you will be tackling this question in the final half-hour of the

2-hour paper. You may be edgy and impatient about getting started. If you can foresee what your problems will be, you will be in a better position to solve them. And the main problem – obviously – is that the poem is 'unseen'. The examiners will be realistic – they understand your situation and will not be expecting a 'perfect' answer.

What *is* expected is that you should attend to the poem carefully. You can be pretty sure that you will not be certain about all aspects of the meaning of the poem. The practice you have done will help you to live with this uncertainty. If you are not sure about the meaning, keep a cool head and make some sensible suggestions. The examiner will be keen to reward you if you can 'think on your feet'.

Regulations
The poem will be printed on the examination paper.

How many marks?
The Unseen Poetry unit (Unit 2: Section C) is worth 10 per cent of the available marks.

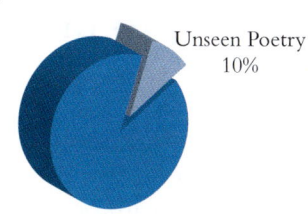

'Quality of written communication'
This is assessed in all units of the examination. You should take care to:

- choose an appropriate form and style for your answer
- organise your material clearly and coherently (e.g. taking care with punctuation and paragraphing)
- write legibly and accurately.

Guide to poetic techniques
The list on the right is intended as a helpful guide to some of the more common poetic techniques. It is *not* a checklist! It is quite possible to express valid ideas without using technical terms but some knowledge of these terms and their use is expected for access to the higher Mark Bands.

How your work is marked
The examiner will be looking for certain key features in your answer:

- **Focus** – Has your response answered the question?
- **Development** – Have you gone into detail?
- **Argument** – Is your response logical and persuasive?
- **Understanding** – Does it show understanding of subject matter and use of language.

These are what you must produce in your answer to ensure success.

Assessment Objectives (AOs)
In this Unseen Poetry unit (Unit 2: Section C), you need to cover the following AOs and demonstrate that you can:

AO1 Respond to texts critically and imaginatively; select and evaluate relevant textual detail to illustrate and support interpretations.

AO2 Explain how language, structure and form contribute to writers' presentation of ideas, themes and settings.

- Comparisons – similes, metaphors, personification
- Imagery and use of the senses – especially visual imagery and aural imagery
- Punctuation – sentence length, line or verse breaks, run-on lines
- Repetition of words or ideas
- 'Sound' features – alliteration and assonance, rhythm, rhyme, repetition, onomatopoeia
- Specific poetic forms – e.g. ode, sonnet, lyric
- Syntax and word order
- Speaker/persona (if used)
- Versification and structure – e.g. couplet, alternate rhyme, octave, iambic rhythm
- Visual impact of the poem on the page

Unseen Poetry 10%

Sample unseen poems

Poems and questions for Foundation and Higher tier

You will be marked out of 20 for these sample questions, which are similar in style to those you will meet in the exam. Remember that the Unseen Poetry question is worth only 10 per cent of the available marks. If you are a Higher tier student and feel that you need more exam practice, it might be useful to begin with Foundation tier questions, which help you to structure your answer, then move on to Higher tier questions when you feel more confident.

'Trying to understand violence'

Context
This poem is by Jenny Joseph. She is a British poet and was born in 1932.

The fly is not a nuisance to itself   1
It is fat and beautiful to its own kind.
Happily it hovers over the meat
Taking off with bounces, buzzing with joy.

In the heat the pavements blotched and stained   5
Stink with the market offal, and the flies
Cluster round the garbage and our legs.
They will choke us if we do not kill them.
Ugh! They are crowding over the food, inserting eggs
Into the meat and smearing it with danger.   10

To hurt humans is quite different, they do not
Rot our substance; the bayonetted babies
And other innocents thrown to the cobblestones
Did not threaten the soldiers; but those men
Had been told they did; taught disgust   15
They swatted them like flies; the eggs would grow
Into a horde to over-run their land.

This sticky gritty wind infects the air
The streets are full of vermin, and ugh! – these flies.

Foundation tier question

See page 176 for a Higher tier question on this poem.

> **F** By referring closely to the details of the poem and particularly to the ways the poet uses language, show what you learn about the speaker's ideas about **violence**.
>
> In your answer you should consider:
>
> (a) the way flies are described in lines 1–4. Discuss the language; [4 marks]
>
> (b) the way the setting is described in lines 5–10, and the feelings of the speaker about it; [4 marks]
>
> (c) what the soldiers in the third section of the poem have been told or taught that **makes** them act as they do; [4 marks]
>
> (d) the comparison in line 16 'They swatted them like flies'. Explain in as much detail as you can what the speaker is saying about violence when she makes this comparison. Do not forget to refer to the ways the poet uses language; [5 marks]
>
> (e) the title of the poem. [3 marks]

Mark Scheme for Foundation tier

Reward answers which can present a personal response and informed argument, backed up with understanding of the poet's methods and intentions.

(a) The description of the flies in lines 1–4

In contrast with later descriptions, the flies are presented as full of the joys of life

Simple, basic description **0–2 marks**

Some development of comments on use of language, e.g. use of word 'bounce', onomatopoeic use of 'buzzing', alliteration on 'happily it hovers' **3–4 marks**

(b) The setting and the speaker's feelings about it in lines 5–10

Simple, basic description **0–2 marks**

Some development of comments, e.g. on words with unpleasant associations – 'stink', 'offal', 'garbage. Use of exclamation to convey disgust.

3–4 marks

> **Checklist**
> Remember to:
> - focus on the question
> - develop the points you make
> - discuss specific uses of language
> - use the name of the poet to help you make points about poetic technique.

(c) What the soldiers have been told or taught that makes them act as they do

The soldiers commit acts of horrible violence, they 'bayonetted babies', as they have been told or taught that these babies and other 'innocents' threaten them.

Simple, basic explanation   **0–1 marks**

Some development of comments, e.g. on the absurdity of the threat, or linking the 'disgust' they have been taught with the disgust of the speaker at the flies, or the link between the flies and the 'innocents' whose eggs would grow   **2–4 marks**

(d) 'They swatted them like flies'

Refers to the actions of the soldiers towards their defenceless victims.

Simple, basic explanation   **0–2 marks**

Some development of comments, e.g. that the violent actions are driven by fear and/or disgust, comment on violence of word 'swat', the soldiers' feelings that they are protecting their land   **3–5 marks**

(e) The poem's title

Reward clarity of discussion in:

the noting of violence as a theme   **1 mark**

reference to the tentativeness of the phrasing of the title – 'trying to understand'   up to **2 additional marks** to a maximum of **3 marks**

Sample upper Band 3 response

> In the poem 'Trying to understand violence', the speaker seems to be attempting to give reasons to explain why people use violence. The poet starts off by talking about flies, which seems strange to the reader because we can't make a link with the title. We wonder what the description of the flies has to do with 'trying to understand violence'.
>
> The first verse describes the fly with words like 'happily', 'joy' and also using onomatopoeia and alliteration – 'bounces, buzzing' which create quite a pleasant image of the flies. I think the way she describes the fly in this verse makes it seem unthreatening and almost appealing.
>
> This changes in the second verse when she starts to use words like 'blotched', 'stained' and 'stink'. These words make us think of decay and rot which is more typically linked to flies. Now the flies seem threatening 'They will choke us if we do not kill them'. I think this is the first link to the title 'trying to understand violence' – people kill flies because if we don't they can spread disease.
>
> There is a sudden change of tone in the third verse when she mentions 'To hurt humans is quite different'. I think she is trying

to make us think about why people hurt others. She is talking about war in this verse 'the soldiers' and gives reasons for why they use violence 'those men had been told' as if they were just following orders. She compares people to flies using a simile 'swatted them like flies' which links the earlier part of the poem with this verse. The excuse the speaker gives for the violence used against these people is that 'the eggs would grow/ Into a horde to over-run their land.' The speaker compares the people this time to the eggs which flies lay and makes them seem like something frightening by using a word like 'horde'. It seems as if she is saying that the soldiers have to use violence to protect their country, just the same as people kill flies to stop disease spreading.

The final section of the poem, which is only two lines long, creates a disgusting image for the reader by using phrases like 'gritty wind which infects the air' and 'the streets are full of vermin' which makes you think of disease. She brings back the image of the flies from the start of the poem, but these flies are not the 'fat and beautiful' one of the first verse, but something disgusting 'ugh! – these flies.'

I think the speaker's ideas about violence are that she is trying to understand why it happens.

Higher tier question

You will find the poem on page 174.

> **H** Write about the poem 'Trying to understand violence'. You should describe what the poet writes about **and** how she uses language to convey her thoughts and feelings.

Sample Band 5 response

The title of the poem is interesting because it suggests that the speaker is going to present an argument to find reasons why violence happens in society rather than clearly express their feelings about violence. The first image in the poem is of a fly which is presented to be harmless and almost comical. The alliteration of 'happily it hovers' and 'bounces, buzzing' creates a pleasant description of the fly. The first verse seems straightforward, but doesn't help the reader understand the speaker's ideas about violence.

Checklist
Remember to:
- plan your answer
- develop the points you make
- discuss specific uses of language
- use the name of the poet to help you make points about poetic technique.

However, this changes in the second verse. The 'fat and beautiful' fly which is 'buzzing with joy' as it goes on its way becomes a swarm. These flies 'cluster round the garbage' and present a problem to 'us'. By using the word 'us' the speaker involves the reader and accurately depicts our disgust at flies by the exclamation 'Ugh!' The speaker creates a vivid image of the flies which are now a threat — 'inserting eggs/ Into the meat and smearing it with danger.' The speaker's ideas about violence here are that it is perfectly justified — everyone kills flies without even thinking because if we don't 'They will choke us'.

The sudden and unexpected change of tone in the third verse surprises the reader. Of course 'To hurt humans is quite different'. Surely no one would see killing flies as the same as killing humans. The speaker's ideas about violence here show through in the use of the alliterative phrase 'bayonetted babies' — the image here is shocking and grabs the reader's attention. This is emphasised by the description of 'other innocents thrown . . . did not threaten'. These innocent victims of violence are not like the flies in the earlier verses — they pose no threat. The violence here seems unacceptable but the speaker goes on to present the reasons why the soldiers attack 'those men had been told'. The speaker is shocked that men can hurt others under orders. These soldiers hadn't been hurt by their victims but carry out their violent acts because they have been 'taught disgust' — they have been told that these are their enemies and must be hated without any personal experience to back this up.

The second and third verses are brought together by the simile 'swatted like flies' where these victims seem to be nothing more to the soldiers than the flies swarming over the meat in the market. The speaker's ideas about violence are shown by the words 'the eggs would grow/ Into a horde to over-run their land.' The fear which is bred into the soldiers gives them excuses for violence against others. Their enemies are a 'horde' which threatens their land.

At the end of the poem, the hatred and disgust which people have for their enemies is shown in the description 'sticky gritty wind infects the air' with its connotations of disease and the ambiguous term 'vermin' — is it referring to the enemy which might 'over-run the land' or the soldiers who carry out these acts of violence? The reader is left with a revolting image of death and disease, highlighted by the repetition of the exclamation 'ugh!'

Overall, I think the speaker's attitude to violence is that it is unjustified. We can't compare humans to flies, but by doing so in the poem, the speaker has shown their contempt for violence.

'Incendiary'

That one small boy with a face like pallid cheese 1
And burnt-out little eyes could make a blaze
As brazen, fierce and huge, as red and gold
And zany yellow as the one that spoiled
Three thousand guineas' worth of property 5
And crops at Godwin's farm on Saturday
Is frightening – as fact and metaphor:
An ordinary match intended for
The lighting of a pipe or kitchen fire
Misused may set a whole menagerie 10
Of flame-fanged tigers roaring hungrily.
And frightening, too, that one small boy should set
The sky on fire and choke the stars to heat
Such skinny limbs and such a little heart
Which would have been content with one warm kiss 15
Had there been anyone to offer this.

Context
This poem is by Vernon Scannell, a British poet who died in 2007.
Note: A guinea is an old unit of money.

Foundation tier question

See page 180 for a Higher tier question on this poem.

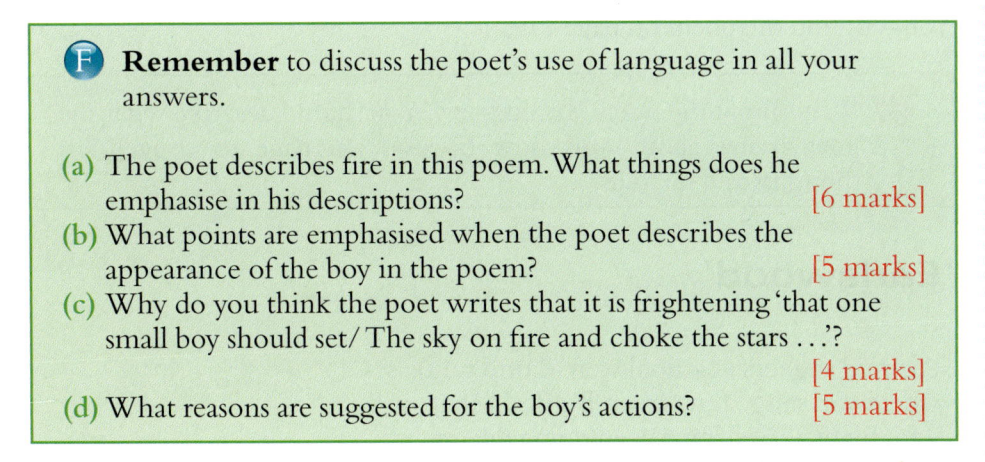

> **F** **Remember** to discuss the poet's use of language in all your answers.
>
> (a) The poet describes fire in this poem. What things does he emphasise in his descriptions? **[6 marks]**
> (b) What points are emphasised when the poet describes the appearance of the boy in the poem? **[5 marks]**
> (c) Why do you think the poet writes that it is frightening 'that one small boy should set/ The sky on fire and choke the stars . . .'? **[4 marks]**
> (d) What reasons are suggested for the boy's actions? **[5 marks]**

Checklist
Remember to:
- answer the question
- develop the points you make
- discuss specific uses of language
- use the name of the poet to help you make points about poetic technique.

Mark Scheme for Foundation tier

Reward answers which can present a personal response and informed argument, backed up with understanding of the poet's methods and intentions.

(a) The description of the fire

Simple, basic elements of description **0–2 marks**

Some comment on noteworthy adjectives such as 'brazen', 'zany'; aural imagery and alliteration involved in the line 'flame-fanged tigers roaring hungrily' **3–6 marks**

(b) The description of the boy

Simple, basic response noting smallness and thinness **0–2 marks**

Some comment on, e.g., paleness, implied lack of attractiveness in simile 'face like pallid cheese', lack of emotion in 'burnt-out little eyes' **3–5 marks**

(c) Why frightening?

For generalised or basic statement that it is frightening because of the damage done **0–2 marks**

For comment on the hyperbole in the lines and/or the discrepancy between on the one hand the magnitude of the deed and the damage ('choke the stars'), and on the other the puniness of the perpetrator **3–4 marks**

(d) Reasons for the boy's actions

Simple, basic explanation based on 'would have been content with one warm kiss' **0–2 marks**

Some comment bringing in use of language, e.g. link with metaphor 'burnt-out little eyes', or repetition of implication that the boy was easily disregarded ('small', 'little', 'skinny'), and/or psychological explanation of actions based on thwarted emotional life of the boy **3–5 marks**

Higher tier question

You will find the poem on page 179.

> **H** Write about the poem 'Incendiary'. You should describe what the poet writes about **and** how he uses language to convey his thoughts and feelings.

'Earlswood'

> Air-raid shelters at school were damp tunnels   1
> where you sang 'Ten Green Bottles' yet again
> and might as well have been doing decimals.
>
> At home, though, it was cosier and more fun:
> cocoa and toast inside the Table Shelter,   5
> our iron-panelled bunker, our new den.
>
> By day we ate off it; at night you'd find us
> under it, the floor plump with mattresses
> and the wire grilles neatly latched around us.
>
> You had to be careful not to bump your head;   10
> we padded the hard metal bits with pillows,
> then giggled in our glorious social bed.

Checklist
Remember to:
- plan your answer
- develop the points you make
- discuss specific uses of language
- use the name of the poet to help you make points about poetic technique.

What could be safer? What could be more romantic
than playing cards by torchlight in a raid?
Odd that it made our mother so neurotic   15

to hear the sirens; we were quite content –
but slightly cramped once there were four of us,
after we'd taken in old Mrs Brent

from down by the Nag's Head, who'd been bombed out.
She had her arm in plaster, but she managed   20
to dress herself, and smiled, and seemed all right.

Perhaps I just imagined hearing her
moaning a little in the night, and shaking
splinters of glass out of her long grey hair.

The next week we were sent to Leicestershire.   25

Context
Fleur Adcock, who wrote this poem, was born in New Zealand in 1934. She was living in England during the bombing raids of the Second World War.

Foundation tier question

See page 182 for a Higher tier question on this poem.

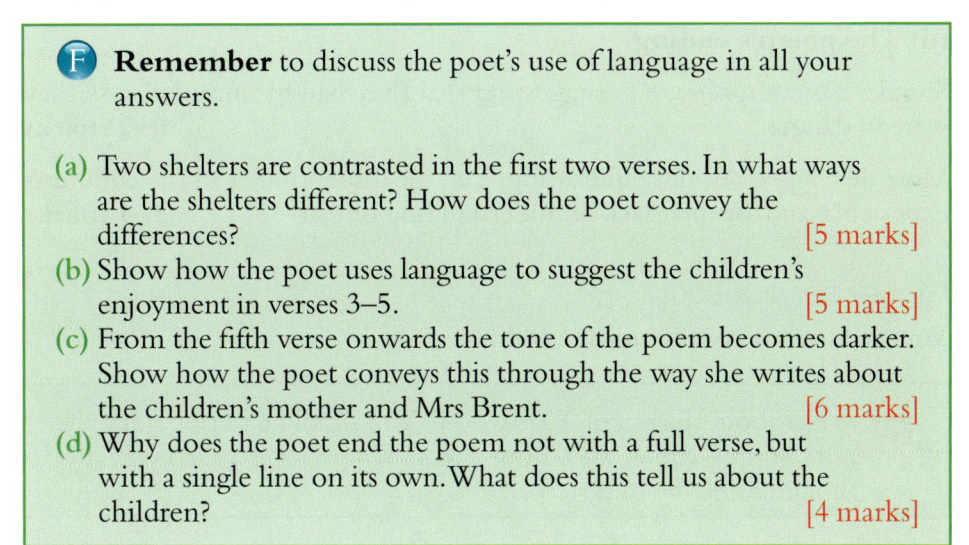

F **Remember** to discuss the poet's use of language in all your answers.

(a) Two shelters are contrasted in the first two verses. In what ways are the shelters different? How does the poet convey the differences? [5 marks]

(b) Show how the poet uses language to suggest the children's enjoyment in verses 3–5. [5 marks]

(c) From the fifth verse onwards the tone of the poem becomes darker. Show how the poet conveys this through the way she writes about the children's mother and Mrs Brent. [6 marks]

(d) Why does the poet end the poem not with a full verse, but with a single line on its own. What does this tell us about the children? [4 marks]

Checklist
Remember to:
- answer the question
- develop the points you make
- discuss specific uses of language
- use the name of the poet to help you make points about poetic technique.

Mark Scheme for Foundation tier

Reward answers which can present a personal response and informed argument, backed up with understanding of the poet's methods and intentions.

(a) The contrasting shelters

Home and school shelters contrasted as regards comfort and enjoyability
1 mark for each factor identified

Up to **3 additional marks** for discussion of language used to convey this contrast: 'damp' v 'cosier and more fun'; dreariness and boredom conveyed through 'yet again' and 'might as well', whereas at home there was the pleasure of 'cocoa and toast'. Repeated use of 'our' suggests proprietorial pleasure.

(b) The children's enjoyment

- Implication in 'you'd find us' that this was a chosen place to be
- Suggestions of security and comfort through vocabulary choices 'plump' and 'neat'
- Suggestion of enjoyable make-do
- Use of words 'giggled' and 'glorious' to suggest their state of mind
- Enjoyment of the unusual, conveyed through rhetorical questions

2 marks for first point made by student; **1 mark for each** additional point to a maximum of **5 marks**.

(c) Change of tone

- The mother's fear of sirens: word choice – 'neurotic'
- Mrs Brent's physical injury: 'arm in plaster'
- Her struggle to dress herself
- Implication in 'seemed all right' that she may not have been
- Speaker's hazy impression of hearing 'moaning'
- Equally hazy impression of actual physical damage and proximity to danger: 'splinters of glass'

Simple, basic response	**0–2 marks**
More developed response commenting on poet's technique	**3–6 marks**

(d) The poem's ending

Simple, basic response, e.g. suggesting that they had to move because they were in danger	**0–2 marks**
More developed response indicating, e.g., the discontinuity of the children's experience and/or their lack of understanding or fear	**3–4 marks**

Higher tier question

You will find the poem on page 180.

> **H** Write about the poem 'Earlswood'. You should describe what the poet writes about **and** how she uses language to convey her thoughts and feelings.

Checklist
Remember to:
- plan your answer
- develop the points you make
- discuss specific uses of language
- use the name of the poet to help you make points about poetic technique.

Poems for further practice at Higher tier

'The Late Wasp'

You that through all the dying summer	1
Came every morning to our breakfast table,	
A lonely bachelor mummer,	
And fed on the marmalade	
So deeply, all your strength was scarcely able	5
To prise you from the sweet pit you had made, –	
You and the earth have now grown older,	
And your blue thoroughfares have felt a change;	
They have grown colder;	
And it is strange	10
How the familiar avenues of the air	
Crumble now, crumble; the good air will not hold,	
All cracked and perished with the cold;	
And down you dive through nothing and through despair.	

Context
This poem is by Edwin Muir, a Scottish poet who lived from 1887 to 1959.
Note: 'Mummers' were actors in traditional folk plays. They appeared only at particular times of the year.

> **H** Write about the poem 'The Late Wasp'. You should describe what the poet writes about **and** how he uses language to convey his thoughts and feelings.

Checklist

- Use of speaker
- Direct address to wasp
- Onomatopoeic effect of rhyme 'summer/mummer', mimicking sound of wasp
- Foreshadowing effect: the 'sweet pit' suggesting the wasp's grave
- Significant rhyme 'older/colder' and later repetition of 'cold'
- Imagery used to describe the air as experienced by the wasp: as 'blue thoroughfares', as something solid, but which is 'crumbling'
- Use of repetition to create an ominous effect
- Discordant sound values in the last line but one
- Long final line representing perhaps the last fall of the dying wasp
- Placing of 'despair' as the final word of the poem
- Any other points

Context
This poem is by Norman McCaig, a Scottish poet who died in 1996.

'Hotel Room, 12th Floor'

This morning I watched from here 1
a helicopter skirting like a damaged insect
the Empire State Building, that
jumbo size dentist's drill, and landing
on the roof of the PanAm skyscraper. 5
But now midnight has come in
from foreign places. Its uncivilised darkness
is shot at by a million lit windows, all
ups and acrosses.

But midnight is not 10
so easily defeated. I lie in bed, between
a radio and a television set, and hear
the wildest of warwhoops continually ululating through
the glittering canyons and gulches –
police cars and ambulances racing 15
to the broken bones, the harsh screaming
from coldwater flats, the blood
glazed on sidewalks.

The frontier is never
somewhere else. And no stockades 20
can keep the midnight out.

> **H** Write about the poem 'Hotel Room, 12th Floor'. You should describe what the poet writes about **and** how he uses language to convey his thoughts and feelings.

Checklist
- Speaker who lies in bed, watches and thinks
- Use of American terms – 'skyscraper', 'sidewalk'
- Place names locating poem in New York
- Simile describing helicopter
- Metaphor describing Empire State Building
- Personification of midnight (and of windows)
- Darkness associated with violence and absence of civilisation
- Shift from visual to aural impressions in second section
- Three-part structure
- Imagery of Indian wars – 'warwhoops', 'stockades', 'canyons and gulches'
- Imagery of city violence – 'blood on pavement'
- Conclusion about violence being found everywhere
- Any other points

Glossary of terms

Ambiguity – having more than one meaning. Ambiguous words or phrases are sometimes used deliberately by writers.

Anticlimax – A disappointing outcome where a climax had been expected.

Aside – A remark made to the audience by a character on stage while they are speaking to other characters.

Characterisation – The ways in which a writer or dramatist conveys information to help the reader or audience form an impression of a character. Can be done through **dialogue**, **imagery** or **direct description** (in novels); or through **dialogue** or direct description in **stage directions** (in plays).

Chronological sequence – The events of a story given in the order in which they would have happened.

Climax – The moment, usually at the end of a novel or play, when the writer or dramatist makes a point most dramatically or most forcefully and memorably.

Dialogue – Conversation between characters in a novel or play, often used as a means of **characterisation**.

Flashback – A scene set earlier than the main action.

Foreshadowing – Giving an indication of an event which is to happen in the future.

Imagery – Language using metaphors, similes and personifications to produce pictures in the reader's or audience's mind.

Narrator – The voice of the storyteller. Can be a character in the story or a so-called 'omniscient narrator' who knows everything about the characters, including their thoughts and feelings.

Plot – The linked sequence of events that forms the storyline.

Props – Objects used onstage by actors.

Set – The scenery used for a play.

Setting – The situation (time and place) in which a story takes place.

Soliloquy – A speech made by a character alone on stage, giving an insight into their inner thoughts.

Stage directions – Instructions in the text to the actor or other theatre people about how a character should be presented or how a particular moment in a play should be managed.

Staging – The dramatic or theatrical techniques used by a playwright.

Structure – The ways in which the various parts of a novel or play are linked together.

Themes – The important issues that a writer/dramatist wants to explore.

Acknowledgements

Unit 1 pages 14, 22 George Orwell, extract from *Animal Farm* (© Martin Secker & Warburg, 1945); **Unit 1 pages 15, 21, 25** Chinua Achebe, extracts from *Things Fall Apart* (© William Heinemann, 1958); **Unit 1 page 20** William Golding, extracts from *Lord of the Flies* (© Faber & Faber, 1954); **Unit 1 pages 21, 24, 27** Harper Lee, extracts from *To Kill A Mockingbird* (© HarperCollins, 1960); **Unit 2A page 67** Arthur Miller, extract from *All My Sons* (Penguin Modern Classics, 2009), © Arthur Miller, 1947; **Unit 2B page 136** John Betjeman, lines from 'In Westminster Abbey' from *Collected Poems* (© John Murray, 1972); **Unit 2B page 139** Louis Simpson, lines from 'The Battle' from *Collected Poems* (© Continuum International Publishers, 1988); **Unit 2B page 141:** Seamus Heaney, lines from 'Death of a Naturalist' from *Death of a Naturalist* (© Faber & Faber, 2006); **Unit 2B page 142** Emily Dickinson, lines from J986/F1096 'A narrow fellow in the grass' from *The Poems of Emily Dickinson*, edited by Thomas H. Johnson (Cambridge, Mass.: The Belknap Press of Harvard University), copyright © 1951, 1955, 1979, 1983 by the President and Fellows of Harvard College; **Unit 2B page 145** Ernest Moll, lines from 'Foxes Among the Lambs' from *Cut from Mulga* (© Melbourne University Press, in association with Oxford University Press, 1940); **Unit 2C page 174** Jenny Joseph, 'Trying to Understand Violence' from *Selected Poems* (© Bloodaxe Books, 1992); **Unit 2C page 179** Vernon Scannell, 'Incendiary' from *Collected Poems 1950-1993* (© Robson Books, 1993); **Unit 2C page 180** Fleur Adcock, 'Earlswood' from *Poems 1960–2000* (© Bloodaxe Books, 2000), reprinted by permission of the publisher; **Unit 2C page 183** Edwin Muir, 'The Late Wasp' from *The Complete Poems of Edwin Muir*, edited by P.H.Butter (© Association for Scottish Literary Studies, 1991); **Unit 2C page 184** Norman MacCaig, 'Hotel Room, 12th Floor' from *The Poems of Norman MacCaig* (© Polygon, 2005).

Photo credits

Introduction piv © 2010 CCEA GCSE Specification in English Literature; **pvi** © Design Pics Inc./Alamy; **Unit 1 p2** © Design Pics Inc./Alamy; **p5** © THE KOBAL COLLECTION/MGM/COOPER, ANDREW; **p7** Tobias Miller – Fotolia; **p9** © Xavier MARCHANT – Fotolia; **p10** © Photos 12/Alamy; **p11** © Peter Stackpole/Time & Life Pictures/Getty Images; **p15** © SSPL/Getty Images; **p17** © Arthur Rothstein/CORBIS; **p23** © Ross Jolliffe/Alamy; **p24** © BGP – Fotolia; **p25** © Mark Atkins – Fotolia; **p26** © UNIVERSAL/THE KOBAL COLLECTION; **p27** © Animal Farm Prods/RGA; **p31** © Design Pics Inc./Alamy; **p32** © Penguin Books Ltd.; **p34** © Faber and Faber; **p36** © The Random House Group Ltd.; **p38** © The Random House Group Ltd.; **p40** © Penguin Books Ltd; **p42** © Penguin Books Ltd; **Unit 2A p44** © Nigel Norrington/ArenaPAL/www.topfoto.co.uk; **p46** © Design Pics Inc./Alamy; **p49** *clockwise l–r* © Faber and Faber; © Pearson Education Ltd.; © Faber and Faber; © Penguin Books Ltd.; © Penguin Books Ltd.; © Penguin Books Ltd.; © Penguin Books Ltd.; © A&C Black; **p50** © COLIN WILLOUGHBY/TopFoto.co.uk; **p51** © Marilyn Kingwill/ArenaPAL/www.topfoto.co.uk; **p52** © BUTLER Henrietta/ArenaPAL/www.topfoto.co.uk; **p53** © Nils Jorgensen/Rex Features; **p54** *t* © SONY PICTURES CLASSICS/THE KOBAL COLLECTION/BRAUN, STEVE, *b* © Donald Cooper/Rex Features; **p56** © Nigel Norrington/ArenaPAL/www.topfoto.co.uk; **p59** *t* © Mark Douet/ArenaPAL/www.topfoto.co.uk, *b* © WILLOUGHBY Colin/ArenaPAL/www.topfoto.co.uk; **p60** © Nils Jorgensen/Rex Features; **p61** © THE KOBAL COLLECTION/PARAMOUNT; **p62** © Rex Features; **p65** © Spice Factory/RGA; **p66** © Robbie Jack/Corbis; **p68** *t* © Photostage, *b* © Nils Jorgensen/Rex Features; **p69** © Geraint Lewis/Rex Features; **p72** © Nils Jorgensen/Rex Features; **p74** © Faber and Faber; **p76** © Penguin Books Ltd.; **p78** © Penguin Books Ltd.; **p80** © Penguin Books Ltd.; **p82** © A&C Black; **p84** © Penguin Books Ltd.; **p86** © Penguin Books Ltd.; **p88** © Penguin Books Ltd.; **Unit 2B p96** © Ingram Publishing Limited; **p99** © Jeremy Woodhouse/PhotoDisc/Getty Images; **p102** © ron – Fotolia.com; **p105** © paul prescott – Fotolia.com; **p107** © PhotoLink/PhotoDisc/Getty Images; **p108** © Geraint Lewis/Rex Features; **p110** © Ingram Publishing Limited; **p112** © Stockbyte/Getty Images; **p114** © Ingram Publishing Limited; **p116** © 1997 Mel Curtis/PhotoDisc/Getty Images; **p118** © PhotoDisc/Getty Images; **p124** © D. Falconer/PhotoLink/PhotoDisc/Getty Images; **p128** © Image Source/Getty Images; **p132** © Luc PATUREAU – Fotolia.com; **p135** © Andreas Stix – Fotolia.com; **p140** © Ingram Publishing Limited; **p144** © Ingram Publishing Limited; **p148** © Snowshill – Fotolia.com; **p151** © Stockdisc/Getty Images; **p153** © Ingram Publishing Limited; **p154** © Michael Homann – Fotolia.com; **p157** © Ingor Normann – Fotolia.com; **p158** © MELBA PHOTO AGENCY/Alamy; **p165** © Ingram Publishing Limited; **p167** © Jim Wehtje/PhotoDisc/Getty Images; **p169** © Image State Media